ID0590825

QUESTIONS AND ANSWERS
ON ENGLISH

Newnes "Q and A" Manuals

QUESTIONS AND ANSWERS
ON ENGLISH

BY

W. J. WESTON, M.A., B.Sc.

GEORGE NEWNES LIMITED
15-17 LONG ACRE
LONDON, W.C.2

Special Edition 1962

Printed in Great Britain by Fletcher & Son Ltd., Norwich.

QUESTIONS AND ANSWERS ON ENGLISH

This little book seeks to help those that are perplexed, as well they may be, by the many peculiarities of our language. To those keenly desirous of speaking and of writing good English doubts and questionings come ever and again. We set out here to resolve the doubts and to answer the questionings,—the ever-recurring ones at any rate.

A or **An**? *Which is the word needed?*

The rule is this: *a* is replaced by *an* before a vowel *sound*. Thus, "An oak is stouter than a beech"; "A. was an apple-pie". This includes words beginning with silent *h*, "Honesty is the best policy; but he who is governed by that maxim is not an honest man". [Mr. Squeers knew this. "But," he said, "when the *h* is sounded, the *a* only is to be used, as a 'and, a 'art, a 'ighway"]; and it is better to extend this to an unaccented syllable beginning with *h*: "an habitual offender", "an hospitable family".

The *sound*, you note, may vary though the same letter represents it: we say "an urn" but "a unique specimen"; we say "an hour" but "a house"; we say "an unusual occurrence" but "a usual thing" (for *usual* begins with a *y* sound). We do find "an unit" "such an one", and so on; but perhaps such expressions sound affected nowadays. This is so in spite of the lines of Browning:

> That low man goes on adding one to one,
>   His hundred's soon hit;
> This high man, aiming at a million,
>   Misses an unit.

and

> All prudent council, as to what befits
> The golden mean is lost on such an one.

The doubt about *a* or *an* comes from the fact that in
their speech people play pranks with their language.
The *n* was once always present. When another consonant sound followed, the *n* of the *an* was at times left
out: *an year* became *a year*. We have forms with and
without *n*, *my* and *mine*, *eve* and *even*, *maid* and *maiden*.
And we have the pet names *Nan* for *mine Ann*, *Ned* for
mine Edward, *Nell* for *mine Ellen*.

Examples: a history, a ewe, a eulogy, a European;
an antique, an hour, an honour, ("For Brutus is an honourable man" and compare "Good luck have thou with
thine honour"). "An historian" and "an historical novel"
are found, the syllable preceded by *an* being unaccented.

Abbreviations. *Shall I use a shortened form?*

The answer seems to be this: if we are quite certain
that our hearers or our readers will readily interpret the
short form in its intended meaning, no harm comes from
its use. If we are not quite certain, we had better write
the full form. Good manners themselves prompt us to
impose no needless burdens upon hearers or readers;
it may well be that, instead of writing A.B.C.A., we
should give ourselves a little more trouble and write
Army Bureau of Current Affairs.

Besides, an abbreviation may be a hidden trap. *Viz*
is one. The full Latin word is videlicet (a word of four
syllables and meaning "one may see"). In *viz* the *z* is the
symbol used by the scribes for *et:* it is not the final letter
of our alphabet. Knowledge of this hardly justifies our
imposing the term on others who may wonder why
they are to pronounce *viz.* as *namely;* that the alternative is *videlicet* may be unconvincing. And yet to pronounce *viz.* as though it rhymed with *fizz* misinterprets
the *z* symbol.

The Army instruction seems applicable to civil life:
"Abbreviations will be used only when there can be no
doubt as to their meaning. The writer of an order, report,

or message is responsible that any abbreviations he may use are such as will be understood by the recipient."

So long as the short form is neither a trap nor an obscurity, it is in the natural development of language. For it conveys thought with greater economy. There seems to be no valid objection to such shortenings as "phone" for "telephone", "photo" for "photograph", "dynamo" for "dynamo-electric-machine", even "gym" for "gymnasium" and "Zoo" for "Zoological Gardens". The great point is that in this matter of language—which concerns others as well as ourselves—we are well advised to conform to custom. We make ourselves a little ridiculous when we insist on "consolidated annuities" though those around us say "consols", or "cinematograph" when others say "cinema", or "costermonger" when others say "coster".

And, since people understand us when we say "bee-bee-see" there is no need to expand into "British Broadcasting Corporation". This last is an illustration of a curious development. A new word is made from the initials of a well-known phrase. We say, "It's a question of £ s. d." (*el-es-dee* not *pounds, shillings and pence*) and "He's an M.P." (an *em-pee* not *a Member of Parliament*).

Accent. *Which is the stressed syllable?*

The general rule for English words is this: the strong accent is nearly always on the first syllable: we say *beáu-ti-ful, sóme-thing, bút-ton, án-im-al.* Occasionally a separable and unstressed syllable comes first: we say *im-méd-i-ate, in-téll-ig-ible.* And when, as we have done so often, we adopt words from other languages the newcomers in time conform to English usage. Thus we hear *cán-ine* more often than *can-íne*, though the latter is nearer to the Latin.

When the same letters stand for both noun and verb, variation in accent allows us at times to discriminate. This word *accent* itself, for instance, has one sound when a noun, another sound when a verb. Used as a noun— "The accent in English words is usually on the first syllable"—we pronounce it *ác-cent*. Used as a verb— "We often accent the verb differently from the noun"— we pronounce it as *ac-cént*. We speak of "a cómpound", but "to compóund a felony"; we give a testimony of good cónduct, we condúct operations with success; we notice a décrease in the number of births, we wisely decréase the errors in our spelling; we make an éxtract of a favourite passage, we ask the dentist to extráct an aching tooth; we compose a dígest of a number of documents, we digést the information gathered.

We may have a similar shifting of the strong accent when the same group of letters is used for both noun and adjective. In the noun the strong accent falls on the first syllable; in the adjective the strong accent falls on a later syllable. Thus, we have *Áu-gust*, the name of the month, and *au-gúst*, the adjective meaning "majestic" or "venerable"; we have the noun *cóm-pact* ("The compact between the parties was scrupulously observed") and the adjective *com-páct*, "knit closely together"; we have the noun *éx-pert* ("The expert gives his evidence clearly") and the adjective *ex-pért*, "skilled", "experienced"; we have the noun *mín-ute* ("Sixty minutes make an hour") and the adjective *min-úte*, "small", "tiny" (change in accent being here accompanied by a change in the vowel sound); and we have the noun *ín-val-id*, the adjective *in-vál-id*.

Adjective: Adverb. *Is the Adjective or the Adverb to be used?*

Shall we say "The snow fell thick" and "The course of true love never did run smooth"? Or shall we replace the adjectives by the adverbs *thickly* and *smoothly*? Say the sentences aloud, and your sense of aptness tells you that the adjectives, not the adverbs, are the words needed. So you will say "This seems conclusive", rightly using the adjective and not the adverb *conclusively*. You say "The butter tastes rancid" and "The milk has turned sour". It would be a quite erroneous devotion to what is supposed to be grammar if we said *rancidly* and *sourly* merely because the words follow the verbs.

At times the one word does duty for both adjective and adverb. As a rule, to be sure, the ending *ly* marks the adverb: *bold* is the adjective, *boldly* the adverb; *high* is the adjective, *highly* the adverb. ("We here highly resolve that these dead shall not have died in vain".) But *ly* is no infallible sign of the adverb. Some adjectives end in *ly*. In "The daily paper" *daily* is an adjective; in "I daily beseech God" *daily* is an adverb. In Wordsworth's "Choice word and measured phrase, a stately speech" *stately* is a descriptive word, an adjective; in Shakespeare's "A figure appears before them, and with solemn march goes slow and stately by them" *stately* is an adverb. *Statelily*, the adverb form, has a terrible sound.

In our proverb, "Fast bind, safe find", *fast* is an adverb. It would be silly to write *fastly*. In "My hard earned wages" *hard* is an adverb; you would be doing yourself injustice if you said "My hardly earned wages". In "Keep right" *right* is the adverb. It would be against English idiom to use *rightly*, though of course *rightly* is the correct word in a sentence like Hamlet's: "Rightly to be great is not to stir without great argument, but greatly to find quarrel in a straw".

Alliteration. *Am I wise in seeking after words with the same opening sounds?*

Perhaps we should not be ever searching. Yet, when they present themselves to us, we need not reject the jingles of like beginnings as mere childish toys. For the alliteration is often very useful, and in more than one way. You remember Mrs. General's advice in *Little Dorrit*. "'Father' is rather vulgar, my dear. The word 'Papa', besides, gives a pretty form to the lips. Papa, potatoes, poultry, prunes and prisms, are all very good words for the lips; especially prunes and prisms." Language is a tool: it is a wonderful means of carrying thought from mind to mind. Language is also a toy: it is a plaything in which from the very beginnings of speech men and women have delighted. And one of the best games you can play with the toy is this gathering together of like sounds. Our proverbs supply many illustrations: "Waste not, want not"; "Penny-wise, pound foolish"; "Be not made a beggar by banqueting upon borrowing".

One example of effective alliteration is in Miss Mitford's contrast of the two cricket umpires. The village team had been beaten; and "A fourth imputed our defeat to the over-civility of our umpire, George Gosseltine, a sleek, smooth, silk, soft-spoken person, who stood, with his little wand under his arm, smiling through all our disasters— the very image of peace and good humour; whilst their umpire, Bob Coxe, a roystering, roaring, bullying blade, bounced and hectored, and blustered from his wicket, with the voice of a twelve-pounder."

Allusion. *Is it well to indulge in allusions?*

Probably not, we should be shy of bringing in allusions as ornaments to our writing. If our hearers or our readers cannot recall it at once, the allusion irritates; if they do recall it, they very likely think it hackneyed and pointless. Mr. Weller had strong views on the matter. "Wot I like in that 'ere style of writin'," said the elder Mr. Weller, "is, that there ain't no callin' names in it,—no Wenuses, nor nothin' o' that kind. Wot's the good o' callin' a young 'ooman a Wenus or a angel, Sammy?"

"Ah! What, indeed?" replied Sam.

"You might just as well call her a griffin, or a unicorn, or a king's arms at once, which is werry well known to be a collection o' fabulous animals," added Mr. Weller.

In one way, no doubt, you are paying a compliment to your hearer or reader. You assume that his knowledge enables him at once to recall the person or place or occurrence to which you allude. But it is foolish to make allusions simply to show off your own knowledge.

American—English. *Is it correct to speak of the "American language"?*

Not at all. The people of Canada and the United States speak English, most of them at any rate. They are all, says Carlyle, "subjects of King Shakespeare". Some divergences from our usage there are; but we have no trouble in reading American books, and not a great deal in interpreting what we hear when the American film is showing.

Some words sound a little strange: *fertile, agile* seem to be pronounced with the short *i* in America; *temporarily* and *primarily* have the accent on *er* instead of on the first syllable; *leisure* rhymes with *seizure*, not with *pleasure*; our *ceremony* (with short *o*) is in America *ceremony* (with long *o*).

Meanings, too, vary in a good many words. *Sweet-shop* is, beyond the Atlantic, *candy store*. And other words may raise a passing doubt: *phonograph* for our *gramophone, fruit pie* for our *fruit tart, collar button* for our *collar stud, cookies* or *crackers* for our *biscuits, muffin* for our *scone* or *tea-cake, suspenders* for our *braces, bill* for our *bank-note, automobile* for our *motor-car, commuters* for our *season-ticket holders*. Such variations, though, only touch the fringe; they do not constitute so great a difference as, say, that between the Northumbrian and the Devonian brands of English.

Analysis. *What is Analysis? Does it help at all in composing English?*

You analyse when you separate a sentence into its

elements; you are thereby able to see clearly the relation of the elements towards one another. This breaking up of the structure is, however, more than a mental exercise. It makes us appreciate good composition; we see the skill shown, and we are impelled to take greater pains with our own composition. Analysis will not by itself make us good composers. It is bound to help, though, provided that we exercise our power to analyse upon instances of good composition.

Analyse, for example, this little paragraph of Macaulay's:

> The mirage misleads the traveller in the Arabian desert. Beneath the caravan all is dry and bare; but far in advance, and far in the rear, is the semblance of refreshing waters. The pilgrims hasten forward and find nothing but sand where, an hour before, they had seen a lake. They turn their eyes and see a lake where, an hour before, they were toiling through sand.

The first sentence—a Simple Sentence it is called—consists of Subject ("The mirage") and Predicate ("misleads . . . desert"). And this Predicate consists of Transitive Verb ("misleads"), Object of Transitive Verb ("the traveller") and of an Extension of the Verb ("in the Arabian desert"). In the second period we have two separate sentences placed in contrast to one another by the conjunction "but". Each part of the Compound Sentence has its Subject ("all" in the first, "the semblance of refreshing waters" in the second) and its own Predicate ("is dry and bare" in the first, "is far in advance and far in the rear" in the second). In the third period we have again a Sentence compounded of two joined by the Conjunction "and", the first a Simple Sentence, the second a Complex Sentence. In the Complex Sentence we have a clause, "Where, an hour before, they had seen a lake" doing duty as an Adverb. The fourth period is similar in structure to the third.

In your analysis you have no need to worry about the appropriate names for the parts into which you dissect the sentence. As good a way of analysing as any—one that most conduces to a thorough understanding—is to isolate the parts while they remain in the sentence. Take this fine sentence from Swift's *Gulliver*:

> He gave it for his opinion, that whoever could make two ears of corn or two blades of grass to grow upon a spot of ground where only one grew before, would deserve better of mankind, and do more essential service to his country than the whole race of politicians put together.

Break it up in some such manner as that below, and you have analysed it adequately for all purposes that matter.

> [He gave it for his opinion] that [whoever could make two ears of corn or two blades of grass to grow upon a spot of ground] [where only one grew before] [would deserve better of mankind] and [would do more essential service to his country] than [the whole race of politicians put together *do*].

Apostrophe. *Which is the recognized way of using the Apostrophe?*

The apostrophe was a printer's device, its purpose being to show that a letter (or letters) had been left out of a word. It still does this in expressions like "I'll see" or "You can't".

The sign was once used in plurals. It is still so used in instances like the following, where its omission might lead to misunderstanding.

There are too many *and's* in the sentence.

Dot your *i's* and cross your *t's*.

The use with the possessive case of the noun at times raises doubts. The old ending to denote the possessive was *es*. The modern representative of this is *'s*; and, wherever we can do so without thereby producing a disagreeable sound, we add the apostrophe followed by the *s* to denote the possessive. Thus, "Mrs. Partington's spirit was up". Consider these:

(1) *The pen of a ready writer* might be put *A ready writer's pen.* [*Writer* is the Singular Noun and we can without difficulty add *'s*.]

(2) *Reference books for writers* might be put *Writers'*

reference books. [Since the plural *writers* already
ends with *s* it would be awkward to add another
s sound.]

(3) *The shop for men* might be put *The men's shop.*
[Here the plural *men* does not end in *s*; we make,
therefore, no disagreeable sound in writing *men's.*]

(4) *The department for ladies* might be put *The ladies'
department.* [The apostrophe alone denotes the
possessive case]

You will notice that the addition of *'s* for the possessive
has no effect on the preceding sound. Contrast the
addition of *s* for the plural: then a preceding sound is
often modified: thus singular *wife* becomes plural *wives.*
But in the possessive the *f* sound remains: thus "Such
was the wife's dowry".

No certainty exists in regard to the use of the apostrophe with proper nouns. You hear in London the full
"St. James's Park", the shorter "St. James' Park"
and the shorter still "St. James Park". Nor can we say
with assurance which of the three is most frequent.

Appropriate Prepositions.   *How can I tell which Preposition to use?*

You can tell this only by observing with care the usage
of good writers and speakers. For here custom decides;
and often no convincing reason can be given for the
custom. For the structure of a word may be no sure guide.
Thus, we have the noun *aversion* (dislike), and this is
built up by the Latin prefix *a* meaning *away* or *from* and
version meaning *turning.* But the preposition *to*, quite as
often as *from* is found with *aversion*, and with the corresponding adjective *averse.* Thus, you have "men averse
from war" but also, in Gray's poem, "What female heart
can gold despise? What Cat's averse to Fish?" Probably
indeed, *aversion to* is found more often than *aversion
from.* It is something, though, to realize that one preposition may be preferable to another. Thus, there is a
difference between "a taste of the pleasures of life" and
"a taste for the pleasures of life"; "a taste of" is a samp-
ling; "a taste for" is a liking, a propensity towards. We

say "agree *with* him and *to* his proposal", but "disagree *with* him and *with* his proposal". We say "To-day's weather is very different *from* yesterday's" but "She showed herself indifferent *to* him".

It is interesting to note how an added preposition can modify the meaning of a preceding verb. Thus, you consult a solicitor when you seek his advice; you consult with your friends when you consider a matter in their company and with their help. You attend church when you go to it; you attend to the sermon when you give your mind to it. You lecture a lazy workman when you reprimand him; you lecture to an appreciative audience when your hearers are interested. You witness an accident; you witness to a man's integrity. You own a book: it is your property. You own to a fault: you acknowledge it. You have finished your paper when you have dealt with it as well as you can; you have finished with your paper when you have read all you care to read.

The list below of the prepositions usually found with certain verbs and adjectives may be useful:
abhorrence of; access to; accommodate to ("you accommodate your mode of living to your income"); accommodate with ("you accommodate him with a loan"); accompanied by ("accompanied by his wife"); accompanied with ("the word was accompanied with a blow"); in accord with; to accuse of; to acquiesce in; adapted to; adept in; affinity to *or* between; averse to; blame for; coincide with; compare with *or* to; compatible with; conformable with; conversant with; correspond with ("A silver penny was supposed to correspond with a penny-weight"); correspond to ("The body corresponds to external conditions"); destitute of; differ from ("One star differeth from another in glory"). But ("You differ with a person"); different from (but *to* is quite usual and is perhaps encroaching); disappointed of ("miserably disappointed of his hopes"); disappointed in ("I am greatly disappointed in him"); divide between ("Divide between self-love and society"); divide among ("He divided Canaan among the Israelites"); emerge from; enjoin upon; foreign to; healed of; hatred of *or* for; impose upon; independent of; militate against; necessary

to; opposite to; prevail upon; reconcile to *or* with; reflect upon; rely upon; replete with; sensible of *but* insensible to; thirst after *or* for.

A or The. *When should I use "a", when "the"?*

Look at these lines of Browning's:

> I promised, if you'd watch a dinner out,
> We'd see truth dawn together—truth that peeps
> Over the glass's edge when dinner's done.

In "a dinner" *a* is the Indefinite Article: *a* or *an* is "one of a number". In phrases like "A penny a mile" and "If two ride on a horse, one must ride behind" you note the old meaning of "one".

In "the glass's edge" *the* is the Definite Article. It is connected with *this* and *that*, and indicates the individual. Of one politician it was said that he was never in want of a word: he always had some word or other at command. Of his rival it was said that he was never in want of the word: he had at command the exact word suited to his purpose. Perhaps the latter is the more valuable asset.

Capitals. *What is the usage in regard to Capital Letters?*

Letters of a larger size and often of a special form are used for several purposes. Like decorative type or italics, capitals may be used as a mechanical device to emphasize, to give an important idea important treatment. Thus: "When the KING and QUEEN were seen in their Coronation Coach near Hyde Park Corner not only by their subjects lining the route, but also by an army of viewers scattered through the Home Counties, it was clear that television was here at last" (*The Times*).

The Capitals—sometimes called Head Letters, or Majuscules—are ordinarily used:

(i) To begin a new sentence;

(ii) To begin a line of poetry;

(iii) To begin a proper name (of day of month, of place, of person). Moreover, the adjectives corresponding

to the proper nouns usually have a capital letter:
British, American, and so on. When, however, the
adjective no longer readily calls up the noun from
which it comes, we have the small letter. Thus
saturnine, jovial, tantalizing do not as a rule have
the capitals.

(iv) When a common noun goes in company with a
proper noun, both nouns have the capital: we
write *River Thames, Herne Bay* and so on; we write
"bishops, priests, and deacons," but "The Bishop
of London". The adjective with the capital also,
as a rule, attracts a capital to its noun. Thus:

> If there is another European War it will differ
> from the Great War at least as terribly as the
> Great War differed from the lesser operations of
> Napoleon.

(v) There is a capital letter for such common nouns as,
being used in a special sense, are understood as
referring to one special person, or place, or thing.
Thus:

> A few days ago the Secretary of the Zoological
> Society challenged the word "rhinoceri" which
> appeared in these columns as a plural of "rhino-
> ceros" (*The Times*).

So in Macaulay's sentence, "Many men of less
parts have reached the Woolsack or the Episcopal
Bench", *Woolsack*, normally a common noun,
becomes a proper noun being used as a summary
of "the honour and power appertaining to the Lord
Chancellor".

(vi) We may speak of an abstract idea as though it
were a person. Then, too, the capital is usual, thus:

> Let not Ambition mock their useful toil,
>   Their homely joys, or destiny obscure;
> Nor Grandeur hear, with a disdainful smile,
>   The short and simple annals of the poor.

(vii) For titles the fashion is to give a capital letter to
each important word: thus *Alice's Adventures in*

> *Wonderland; The Taming of the Shrew; The Decline
> and Fall of the Roman Empire.*

(viii) The convention in regard to capitals at the opening
and closing of a letter is this: capitalize each word
of the opening—*My Dear Sir*; capitalize the first
and the last words of the closing—*Your obedient
Servant.*

The use of capitals—like the use of decorative type or
of italics—is a mechanical device for giving to an important idea important treatment. Former writers (or
printers) made great use of the initial capital. In the first
printing of *L'Allegro*, for instance, you have:

> Haste thee nymph, and bring with Thee
> Jest and youthful Jollity,
> Quips and cranks and wanton Wiles,
> Nods, and Becks, and wreathed Smiles.

The modern printer seems to work on the rule, "When in
doubt use lower case"—use the small rather than the
capital letter.

Case. *Should this Pronoun be in the Nominative or in the Objective Case?*

English still retains different forms for the different
cases of pronouns: *I, we, he, she, they, who,* for the nomi-
nátive (the subject of the sentence), *me, us, him, her, them,
whom* for the objective (the object of the sentence).
Trouble arises at times when a pronoun follows what is
called a copulative (or joining) verb: if the nominative
precedes the nominative should also follow. Thus: "It is
he that is the culprit" (not *him*). "Is she as tall as me?"
asks Cleopatra in the play. Strict grammar would have
"Is she as tall as I?"

Since the relative pronoun *who* or *whom*, comes as a
rule, at the beginning of its clause, we need to exercise
care in determining whether the nominative or the objective is needed. Thus consider this sentence: "Here is the
man . . . I saw". Clearly, the pronoun to fill the blank is the
object of the verb *saw*: it must therefore be *whom*. But

in the sentence, "Here is the man . . . saw me", the pronoun to fill the blank is the subject (nominative case,
that is) of the verb *saw*: it must therefore be *who*.

Circumlocution. *Is the straightforward or the roundabout way the better?*

Almost always the first. The ancient advice is "Let
thy speech be short, comprehending much in few words".
The roundabout way—the circumlocution or the peri-
phrasis it may be called—has its uses it is true; but the
single word is usually more effective than its expanded
substitute. On the statue of Mr. Pitt in the London
Guildhall the inscription ended "He died poor". There
can be no doubt that this straightforward, simple expression is better than the suggested "He expired in neces-
sitous circumstances". It is better to say "Cheshire
cheese" than "That which Cestria sends, Tenacious paste
of solid milk".

Yet a circumlocution may be attractive as with Wordsworth's robin, "The pensive warbler of the ruddy breast",
or his cuckoo, "Blithe newcomer, darling of the spring",
or his skylark, "Ethereal minstrel! pilgrim of the skies".
And politeness may prompt a change from the simple,
downright term to the tactful roundabout. "This per-
version of the truth can deceive no one" says *The Times*.
"This lie" may have been too blunt. In his very early days
as a Minister of the Crown, Mr. Churchill had to deal with
the question of why the Government had lied in regard
to native labour. "It cannot," he said, "in the opinion
of His Majesty's Government be classified as slavery in
the extreme acceptance of the word without some risk of
terminological inexactitude." The circumlocution, we
are to suppose, was preferable to a blunt confession of
fault. The preacher at Whitehall was perhaps well
advised when he ended his sermon with a score of words
instead of two: "In short," he said, "if you don't live
up to the precepts of the Gospel but abandon yourselves
to your irregular appetites, you must expect to receive
your reward in a certain place which 'tis not good manners
to mention here." And sometimes the roundabout way

may be great fun. Says Falstaff, "I may truly say with the hook-nosed fellow of Rome, 'I came, saw, and over-came'". The fat knight turned even mighty Caesar into laughter.

Collective Nouns. *Does a Noun, the name of a group of individuals, take the singular or the plural of the Verb?*

A number of individuals, united in some way or other, may have a special name. Cobbett's whimsical collection of instances is, "Names of number, or multitude, such as *Mob*, Parliament, Rabble, House of Commons, Regiment, Court of King's Bench, Den of Thieves, and the like".

In strictness such a noun, a *crew*, a *committee*, a *crowd*, a *congregation*—a collective noun it is called—is in the singular, and its verb should be singular: "The crew is inspected", "The committee considers", "The congregation remains seated". You may, however, have prominent in your mind the many individuals making up the group; and you very naturally slide into the plural for the verb or the pronoun. In modern usage, indeed, the plural is found more-often than the logical singular: we have "The Committee are agreed upon their findings" rather than "The Committee is agreed upon its findings".

The fact that the collective noun may, quite in accordance with good usage, be treated either as a singular or as a plural suggests a caution: we should be consistent in the matter. Here are two sentences from Matthew Arnold: "In our race are thousands of readers, presently there will be millions, who know not a word of Greek and Latin, and will never learn these languages. If this host of readers are ever to gain any sense of the power and charm of the great poets of antiquity their way to gain it is through the original power of Milton." Now, "this host of readers" treats *host* as a singular; but "are ever to gain" treats *host* as a plural. Or perhaps *readers* has attracted the verb into the plural. At any rate the expression is awkward.

Comma (Enumerations). *In making an enumeration should a comma precede "and"?*

The practice of *The Times* has much to commend it; the comma is used to separate the items of an enumeration even though *and* follows the comma. Thus, speaking of the mounting of the guard by the Dominion troops: "To-day, to-morrow, and Thursday, Australian, New Zealand, and South African troops will continue the innovation begun yesterday by the Canadians." So in this sentence from Morley's *Life of Gladstone*, "The letters show how the burden of men is made heavier by slovenly dates, illegible signatures, and forgetfulness that writing is something meant to be read". Look at the punctuation in these lines of Masefield's:

> Then hey for croft and hop-yard, and hill, and field, and pond,
> With Bredon Hill before me and Malvern Hill beyond;
> The hawthorn white i' the hedgerow, and all the spring's attire
> In the comely land of Teme and Lugg, and Clent, and Clee, and Wyre.

Comparison (Adjectives and Adverbs). *What are the rules about comparison?*

Some descriptive adjectives do not admit of more or less: a thing is either *wooden* or *not wooden*. So with adjectives like *weekly, unique, circular, dead, Russian, real, impossible, excellent*. The last word *excellent*, for instance, means "surpassing in some good quality"; that is, it already makes a comparison. "A most excellent dinner" is, therefore, not a good substitute for "A very good dinner". *Ideal*, again, means in ordinary language, "such as cannot be improved upon". "An ideal solution" is as strong as possible: to add *most*, as in the sentence below, is to paint the lily:

> "To allow of exclusion by county majorities appears, then, a most ideal solution of these difficulties."

Other adjectives and some adverbs do admit of more

or less. In comparing *two* things we use what is called the Comparative Degree; and this is usually denoted by the adding of *er* or the prefixing of *more* to the simple form of the adjective or adverb. Thus: "Heard melodies are sweet, but those unheard are sweeter." When *more than two* things enter into the comparison we use what is called the Superlative Degree; and this is usually denoted by the adding of *est* or the prefixing of most to the simple form. Thus: "Clunton and Clunbury, Clungunford and Clun, are the quietest places Under the sun."

The Superlative, however, is quite often used when the comparison is only implied: it is in fact used for emphasis. Thus, the pedantic lady was not justified in finding fault with her husband's "My Dearest Maria". Her reply opened with the request, "My Dear John, I beg that you will mend either your morals or your grammar. You call me your *dearest* Maria; am I to understand that you have other Marias?" But John had abundant authority for using *dearest* in the sense of *very dear*.

Some of our older words have different words for the different degrees: *good*, *better*, *best*; *bad* or *ill*, *worse*, *worst*; *little*, *less*, *least*, and so on.

When the adjective or the adverb contains several syllables the prefixing of *more* or *most* is usually preferred to the adding of *er* and *est*. Thus: "The most formidable weapon", "A more lively engagement". And, now and then, you will find both ways of denoting comparisons: thus "After the most straitest sect of our religion I lived a Pharisee", and "This was the most unkindest cut of all".

Comparisons introduced by *than* and *like* and *as* need care. Consider, for example, this sentence:

The Nile is said to be longer than all rivers in the eastern hemisphere.

Wouldn't it be better to insert *other* before *rivers*?

But *others* is a quite needless insertion in:

The expedient would lead to a state of affairs of all others the most calamitous. [Better write "the most calamitous of all".]

And you agree that the sentence below, as it stands, is nonsense:

This is the character that of all others appeals most to the sympathies.

Like as an adjective, is equivalent to *similar to*. The pronoun following it is, therefore, in the objective case. "He is like me in this" is correct. When the conjunction *as* ushers in a comparison, the following pronoun may be in the nominative case. Thus: "He does it as I do."

Would you care to criticize and to amend the defecti sentences below:

   (i) We are met together on a rather unique occasion.
  (ii) This course of action is more preferable than the other.
 (iii) Thou art a girl as much brighter than her.
       As he was a poet sublimer than me.
  (iv) He finished the work like he had been ordered to do.
   (v) Nothing has happened to me but what has happened to men much better than me.
  (vi) I do now publish my Essays; which, of all my other works, have been most current; for that, as it seems, they come home to men's business and bosoms.

Compound Words (Hyphens). *When is it desirable to use a hyphen in a compound word?*

Compound words go through three stages. Two or more separate words often come together: *a public house, a tobacco pouch.* Constant union brings a hyphen to join them: *a lift-man, a wrist-watch, to-day, brother-in-law.* Finally the two words merge into one and the hyphen disappears: *playmate, handkerchief.* But consistency is absent: thus, Tennyson has "Jewels five-words long That on the stretched fore-finger of all time Sparkle for ever". But you will probably find *forefinger* more often without the hyphen. These notes may help towards consistency in use:

   (1) The hyphen is a symbol whereby, for a particular

purpose, words are made into one: as *apple-tree* (the first of the compound denoting kind), *grass-green*, *penny-wise*, *pound-foolish*, *man-of-war*.

(2) The novelty being gone we omit the hyphen unless (as in *father-in-law*) the resulting word is too cumbrous: write *blackbird*, *whitewash*, *overcome*, *barefoot*, *scarecrow*, *spendthrift*, *outlive*. This is particularly so when it is not at once apparent that the word is a compound: thus *gospel* (*good-spell*, i.e. *good tidings*), *daisy* (*day's eye*), *holiday* (*holy-day*), *Christmas* (*Christ's-mass*).

(3) Omit the hyphen when the words may stand alone: write "*The Major General*" but "*Major-General Dawkins*"; write "*The Solicitor General*" but "*The Solicitor-General's contentions*"; write "*The Court Martial was convened*" but "*The Court-Martial's decision will be promulgated*".

(4) Where there is a single strong accent on the first syllable the word is entire: *waterfront*, *downfall*, *breakfast*, *makeshift*, *masterpiece*, *spellbound*. Contrast words like *grass-grown*, *purse-proud*, *long-haired*, *kill-joy*, *coach-house*.

Note how the hyphen will sometimes prevent mis-understanding. Thus, we had better have a hyphen between *light* and *house* in "She was a light house keeper's daughter", one between *low and scoring* in "a low scoring game" (speaking of a cricket-match), one between *rain* and *swept* in "Scene is rain swept Downing Street".

Conjunctions. *Is it usual to begin a sentence with a conjunction?*

It is not usual, and some consider it a blemish so to begin. The practice of good writers, and of good speakers, gives, however, no support to the objection. And, after all, if your writing is to be a well-linked whole, there must be some way or other of carrying on the thought from one sentence to the next. One might contend, therefore, that the beginning of a sentence is a quite natural place for the conjunction. In speaking—in telling a story especially—it is the natural way to add a sentence to its forerunner by a conjunction. Look at the closing paragraph of *David Copperfield:* the first three sentences all begin with conjunctions:

> And now, as I close my task, subduing my desire to linger yet, these faces fade away. But one face, shining on me like a heavenly light, by which I see all other objects, is above them and beyond them all. And that remains. I turn my head and see it, in its beautiful serenity, beside me. My lamp burns low and I have written far into the night; but the dear presence, without which I were nothing, bears me company.

Here are two little paragraphs of Macaulay. Notice, in the first that *and, but,* and *if* begin sentences, and that *but* links the second paragraph to the first:

> As an observer of life, of manners, of all the shades of human character, he stands in the first class. And what he observed he had the art of communicating in two widely different ways. He could describe virtues, vices, habits, whims, as well as Clarendon. But he could do something better. He could call human beings into existence, and make them exhibit themselves. If we wish to find anything more vivid than Addison's best portraits, we must go either to Shakespeare or to Cervantes.
>
> But what shall we say of Addison's humour, of his sense of the ludicrous, of his power of awakening that sense in others, and of drawing mirth from incidents which occur every day and from little peculiarities of temper and manner, such as may be found in every man? We feel the charm: we give ourselves up to it; but we strive in vain to analyse it.

Conjunctions (CORRELATIVES). *Are there any idioms in English concerning conjunctions?*

Yes: two peculiarities need notice. The first is that certain words ask to be followed by a special companion, a correlative it is sometimes called. Thus *though* requires *yet* ("Though deep, yet clear; though gentle, yet not dull"); *whether* requires *or; either* requires *or; neither* requires *nor; more* requires *than; such, as,* and *so* require *as.* It is awkward, therefore, when words in a sentence call for different correlatives. This sentence of Mills', for instance, can be improved:

> The natural agent is indeed as indispensable (and even more so) as any implement.

As indispensable calls for *as, more so* calls for *than.* It would be better to make the parenthesis into a following sentence: "It is even more indispensable [than any implement]."

The second peculiarity is the occasional omission of the conjunction *that:* "He promised he would soon return." Here no difficulty arises in supplying the omission. In a sentence like the following, however, it would perhaps be better to write *that* after *assume:*

> We assume in the interest of the community you will serve.

Context. *Does its context affect the meaning and the use of a word?*

In English the context of a word determines, to a very great extent, both meaning and use. An English word is not a rigid thing; it takes on differing shades of meaning, it actually changes from one "part of speech", in accordance with differing contexts. Look at an example or two. *Word* is usually a noun. It becomes a verb in Cleopatra's comment after listening to her conqueror's honeyed speech:

> He words me, girls, he words me, that I should not
> Be noble to myself.

The word *after* may signify "behind in place or order": it is then an adverb, as in "Jack fell down and broke his crown, and Jill came tumbling after" and "They lived happily ever after". *After* is also a preposition, taking a noun or pronoun in the objective case, in sentences like "After me cometh a man that is preferred before me", "Wolsey was greedy after power", "Make enquiry after his health". *After* is also a conjunction, joining a dependent clause to its principal clause, in sentences like: "We had a pleasant evening after that wretched fellow went away", "Make your decision only after you have heard both sides of the argument."

Nor do these three exhaust the changes. *After* is a descriptive word, an adjective that is, in phrases like "the after deck", "in after life", "such a scene as no after events have been able to efface". *After* may even be used as a verb as in "After him then, and bring him back".

So, too, you should shrink from defining a word in isolation. For, when a word has long been current among us, it is apt to take on differing shades of meaning, shades determined by the context. How do you interpret *fast* in these two sentences, "Stand fast in the faith", and "Is this a slow or a fast train"? You interpret *fast* in the first sentence as "fixed, firm, constant", the meaning in phrases like the Navy's "Make fast", in "fast aground" and in "Britain and America must be fast friends".

In the second sentence, though, you interpret *fast* as "rapid in movement" not "fixed, stationary". You see how the curious divergence has come about. It calls for strength to stand fast in a position from which people are striving to oust you. But the strength enabling one to stand firm implies the strength to move, to move moreover with speed.

Custom in Language, *Is it wise to conform to custom in language?*

Certainly: custom is the mistress of language; where custom speaks it is unwise to disregard it in view of an assumed greater correctness. Thus, we had better go with the crowd and say *sin-em-a* (*cinema*), even though we still retain, in the less used but corresponding adjective, the *k* sound and the long *i*—*kin-et-ic*. For knowledge of a word's forerunner is no infallible guide to present pronunciation, or present use. Thus *deficit* (with the short *e* and the accent on the first syllable) is the customary (and therefore "correct") though Latin suggests a long *e* and the accent on the second syllable. We had better say *agent* and *alien* (with long *a*) though the Latin *a* is short, *comic*, *echo*, *ethics*, *editor* (short vowels) though in the classic languages the vowels were long, even *patriot* (with long *a*) though the Latin is short, as it is in *paternoster*.

Dash (Punctuation). *When is the dash used in punctuation?*

Its chief use is to mark off an insertion—a parenthesis it is called—in a sentence. Thus in Hamlet's question:

> Who would fardels bear,
> To grunt and sweat under a weary life,
> But that the dread of something after death,—
> The undiscovered country from whose bourn
> No traveller returns,—puzzles the will?

So used it may be replaced by brackets (   ), or, when the parenthesis is only short by commas   ,   ,.
The dash also serves to indicate an abrupt pause in the sentence. Thus:

As soon as we two were alone—"What," said Prince Florizel, "is the use of this confabulatioñ, Geraldine? I see you are flurried, whereas my mind is very tranquilly made up. I will see the end of this."

Detached Phrase (Nominative Absolute). *Is the Pronoun in a detached phrase Nominative or Objective?*

In the Nominative; for the use of a noun or pronoun with a participle is a substitute for an inserted sentence. Thus, in the lines:

> Here with a Loaf of Bread beneath the Bough,
> A Flask of Wine, a Book of Verse—and thou
>   Beside me singing in the Wilderness—
> And Wilderness is Paradise enow.

it is *thou* (not *thee*) in the phrase. The grammarian speaks of *thou* in such a phrase as being in the Nominative Absolute. So in the question, "I being a poor man and he being a millionaire, which of us will she choose?" it is *I* and *he* (not *me* and *him*).

Dilemma ("Horns of a Dilemma"). *Is "Dilemma" simply another word for "Confusion" or "Perplexity"?*

"Dilemma" is very often used as a variant for "confusion" or "perplexity" ("I had left my money at home and was therefore in a dilemma"). The fit use of "dilemma", however, is to signify a forced choice between two courses, both courses being disagreeable or dangerous or unprofitable. "We must hang together, or hang separately", says the ruffian: we must either stick to the gang, much as some of us dislike their ways, or we shall be taken by the police and be deservedly hanged. The disagreeable alternatives are the "horns of the dilemma". A good instance is this from *Tristram Shandy*:

Yorick was cutting the manuscript of his sermon into slips so that the company might light their pipes. This annoyed *Didius*:

"If the sermon is of no better worth than to light pipes with—'twas certainly, Sir, not good enough to be preached before so learned a body; and if 'twas good enough to be preached before so learned a body—'twas certainly, Sir, too good to light their pipes with afterwards".

"I have got him fast hung up", quoth *Didius* to himself, "upon one of the two horns of my dilemma —let him get off as he can."

"I have undergone such unspeakable torments in bringing forth this sermon," quoth *Yorick* upon this occasion,—"that I declare, Didius, I would suffer martyrdom before I would sit down and make such another: it came from my head instead of my heart— and it is for the pain it gave me, both in the preaching and writing of it, that I revenge myself of it in this manner.—To preach, to show the extent of our reading, or the subtleties of our wit—to parade in the eyes of the vulgar with the beggarly accounts of a little learning, tinselled over with a few words that glitter, but convey little light and less warmth—is a dishonest use of the poor single half-hour in a week which is put into our hands."

Direct Speech (Oratio Recta) and **Reported Speech** (Oratio Oblique). *How is the distinction between these shown?*

Direct Speech consists of the actual words used, or supposed to be used, by a speaker. Reported Speech is such an account of this Direct Speech as might be preceded by "He said". In writing we mark off the actual words spoken by inverted commas. Thus:

"It is kind of you to come back to us, Henry," Lady Esmond said, "I thought you might come." "We read of the fleet coming to Portsmouth. Why did you not come from Portsmouth?" Frank asked.

We turn the direct speech into reported speech by changing the tense of the verbs and the persons of the pronouns. Thus:

Lady Esmond said that it was kind of him to come back to them. She had thought he might come. Frank said that they had read of the fleet coming to Portsmouth. and asked why he had not come from Portsmouth.

Note that the mark of interrogation does not follow the reported question. Thus: "Is that the man you saw?" *but* He asked whether that was the man he had seen.

Doubled Consonants. *Have we any rule when to use a Double Consonant?*

We have no reliable rule: we must trust to careful observation if we are to spell in accordance with custom. Sound is no good guide; for we have *committee* and *comity* ("The comity of nations implies a courteous recognition of each other's laws"), we have *levelled* and *paralleled*, *Britain* and *Brittany*.

There is something of a rule when an inflexion (like *ed* or *est*) is added:

(1) We double the final consonant when the original is a single syllable or when the final syllable is accented: *pot* becomes *potted*, *knot* becomes *knotted*; *regret* becomes *regretted*, *demur* becomes *demurred* and *demurrage*.

(2) We double the *l* preceded by a single vowel: *level* becomes *levelled*, *control* becomes *controllable*, *jewel*

becomes *jewellery.* We keep the *l* single when the preceding vowel is double: *fail* becomes *failure, boil* becomes *boiler.* (American usage has no such distinction, *travel* becomes *traveler*; and we copy in these words the American usage, *almighty, almost, already, always, wilful*).

These are the words that give most trouble: *accommodation* (two *c*'s, two *m*'s), *abbreviation, all right* (and note the distinction between "They came all together" and "It is altogether wrong to do this"), *battalion* (one *l*), *camellia, desiccated* (i.e. dried, one *s*, two *c*'s), *moccasins, exaggerate, woollen* (but American usage prefers *woolen*), *skilful, fulfil, until.*

Double Plurals. *Are the Alternative Plurals of some Nouns of any use?*

Well, there is something of an economizing instinct in language; and when two words exist for the one idea, they come in time to express differing shades of meaning. Thus, there is the foreign plural of *index (indices,* that is); and *indices* is the term for figures like the 3 in 4^3, indicating how many times we are to use 4 as a factor. The English plural, *indexes,* is kept for alphabetical lists of the topics dealt with in a book. So, too, *geniuses* (plural of *genius*) are people having extraordinary capacity; and *genii* (the alternative plural) are the wonder-working spirits of fairy-tales. We use *pence* (as plural of *penny*) when we have a collection in mind ("Take care of the pence and the pounds will take care of themselves"); we use *pennies* when we have the individual coins in mind ("For a long period of our history silver pennies constituted the currency"). *Brothers* is the ordinary plural; *brethren* is for the pulpit or the platform.

Double Possessive. *What is the explanation of the Double Possessive we find at times?*

The opening sentence of *Antony and Cleopatra*—"Nay, but this dotage of our general's o'erflows the measure"— and the expression "He's always poking that nose of his into other people's business" are instances of this idiom.

The common explanation, that "a poem of Browning's"
is a shortening of "a poem from among Browning's
poems", can hardly be correct. The explanation certainly
would not fit "that nose of his", for he has but one nose.

Of here ushers in a parallel expression: "This son of
mine" is another way of saying "This, my son". Note
how the idiom enables us to distinguish between ideas.
"An impartial judgment of him" is a judgment *about*
him. "An impartial judgment of his" is a judgment *by*
him. "A friend of Tom's" is one whom Tom likes, "a
friend of Tom" is one who likes Tom. "A picture of the
King" is the King's likeness; "a picture of the King's" is
a picture belonging to him.

Compare "The Island of Cyprus" (i.e. "The Island,
Cyprus") and "The City of York" (i.e. "The City named
York").

Doublets and Triplets. *How comes it that we have
in English two or more words from the one
original?*

The words have come into our language at different
times and, quite likely, by different ways—one of the
group by way of speech, one by way of writing. Introduced by way of writing, by copying from the original,
the word keeps close to its origin; introduced by way of
speech the word tends to diverge greatly. The Latin, for
instance, is *abbreviationem*: importation by way of writing
gives us *abbreviate*, importation through speech gives us
abridge. The Latin *redemptionem* gives us, in like
manner, the written *redemption*, the spoken *ransom*.
Pauperem gives *pauper* and *poor*, the first transferred by
writers from book to book, the second among the dona-
tions of the Normans to our language.

Other pairs are *captive* and *caitiff*, *diurnal* and *journal*,
secure and *sure*, *fragile* and *frail*, *hotel* and *hospital*—
these from a Latin origin. Pairs from a common Greek
origin are *scandal* and *slander*, *blaspheme* and *blame*,
phantasy and *fancy*, *balsam* and *balm*, *iota* and *jot*.

Instances where more than two words from the one
origin exist are not uncommon. Greek *diskos* (the

Discobolos is the quoit-thrower) has given us *disc* (a round plate), *dais* (the raised floor in a hall), *desk* (a sloping table), and *dish* (a platter)—the things named resembling one another in little more than in each having a flat surface. *Dame, dam, donna, duenna* all diverge from the Latin *domina*, as *sir, sire, senor, senior* do from the Latin *senior*. *Leal, loyal, legal; card, chart, carte; ration, ratio, reason; plan, plane, plain*—these are other triplets from the one original.

It will not be overlooked that divergence in meaning or in application has come along with divergence in form: a man may be poor without being a pauper.

E (Silent or Mute). *Why do we keep the silent* e *in English words?*

For these purposes:

(1) To indicate that the preceding word is long, *wine, paste, bite, rode* (contrast *win, past, bit, rod*—all with short vowels).

(2) To indicate that *v* is a consonant, not a vowel: *live, have, love, gave, brave*. (In early printing *live* was *liue*. It is because of this device that no English word ends in *v*; for, of course, a word like *Slav* is not really English.)

(3) To indicate that *c* is sounded as *s* not as *k*: *nice, defence, twice* (contrast *tic-tac*).

(4) To indicate that *g* has the soft sound: *drudge, bridge, age, rage* (contrast *drug, brig, rag*).

(5) To indicate French origin: *choice, grimace, caprice, police, foible*. But the caprice of printers dictates many of our spellings: *are, were, come, one, none*; there is *Magdalen* College at Oxford, *Magdalene* College at Cambridge; and *judgement* competes with *judgment, moveable* with *movable, loveable* with *lovable*.

Notice *gaugeable, noticeable, enforceable, singeing*, when the *e* is retained to indicate that *g* and *c* have the soft sounds.

Exclamation Mark. *When is this mark appropriate?*

The Exclamation Mark—at times called "Mark of Admiration"—is correctly used with genuine exclamations. Thus in Shelley's lines:

> O World! O Life! O Time!
> On whose last steps I climb,
> Trembling at that where I had stood before;
> When will return the glory of your prime?
> No more,—Oh, never more!

The *O* in *O World!* is a call for attention; the *Oh* in *Oh, never more!* is a cry of pain. The mark guides the reader and asks him to express the strong feeling of the writer. A good illustration is this from Trevelyan's *History of England:*

> Six years after Poitiers a statute was passed through Parliament declaring that since the French tongue was "much unknown in this Realm", all pleading and judgments in the law courts should be spoken in the English tongue and enrolled in Latin. "Men of law fro that tyme should plede in her moder tunge," it was said. "Their mother tongue!" Here indeed is a new and significant order of ideas! If the statute was imperfectly obeyed at first, it was obeyed before long, although lawyers, with professional conservatism, long continued to write documents in the "law French" in which their predecessors had addressed the court.

As will be seen from the instance after *ideas* above, the mark is at times used in order to make a statement emphatic. Note the distinction:

Smith has scored. (A matter of fact statement).
Smith has scored? (A request for information).
Smith has scored! (An exclamation of delight, or of amazement).

Figures of Speech. *What is Figurative Language?*

We may relinquish strict accuracy in our speech or our writing in order to make that speech or writing more impressive or more picturesque. We leave the literally true and say what is true only by way of comparison. So doing we use figurative (or metaphorical) language. Thus, Charles Lamb complains, perversely very likely, of a Scotsman: "You must speak upon the square with him. He stops a metaphor like a suspected person in an enemy's country. 'A healthy book!'—said one of his countrymen to me, who had ventured to give that appellation to *John Buncle*—did I catch rightly what you said? I have heard of a man in health, and of a healthy state of body, but I do not see how that epithet can be properly applied to a book."

Those cards, for instance, that usurp so much time of so many of us may serve as implied illustrations, as figurative language that is. We may speak of an unsafe plan as "a house of cards"; we "throw in our cards" when we abandon the plan; "we play our cards well" when we make the best of things; we "show our cards" or "put our cards on the table" when we reveal our strength; we have "a sure card" when we have at our disposal what will command success.

So, too, crowds of our expressions bear witness to the influence of the sea upon our national life, and therefore national language. A political party looks for a "turning of the tide", hopes that fortune is now "at the lowest ebb", trusts that "tiding over their present setback" their success will soon be "at the height". We "sail in troubled waters" when things are going badly for us, we are "at sea" in a rudderless boat when perplexed; we console ourselves by the thought "There are just as good fish in the sea"; we "drown our sorrow" at the "shipwreck of our hopes", becoming indeed "half seas over"; we "take in sail" when we moderate our ambitions; we trust that at length "our ship will come home" and we reach "the haven where we fain would be".

Foreign Terms. *How far is it advisable to use Foreign Words and Phrases?*

Consideration of this fact leads to the answer: Language is a matter of co-operation; we make certain sounds with our vocal organs or we make certain black signs on white paper, and we ask another to interpret those sounds or signs. Prudence dictates that we should not ask too much from our interpreter. We should use only such terms as we are tolerably certain he can interpret without trouble; we are not to use foreign terms, or indeed any terms, foreign or not, mainly in order to show off our great learning.

In other words we are to be most sparing in our use of foreign terms. We might well imitate Fuller's *Good Schoolmaster*, "Out of his school he is no way pedantic in carriage or discourse; contenting himself to be rich in Latin, though he doth not jingle it in every company wherein he comes". Yet we must remember that many foreign importations have become a real and useful part of the English language. This is so even though we write them in italics, and perhaps make brave efforts to pronounce them as we think they are pronounced elsewhere. Thus a *pied-à-terre* is more than "a foot on the ground", a person's *bête noire* more than his "black beast"; to give one *carte blanche* is a very effective way of saying "to give unlimited discretion"; *dilettante* is better than "smatterer' and "evening dress is *de rigeur*" is perhaps better than "evening dress is required by etiquette".

Look at four instances from Professor Trevelyan's *History of England*: you will probably agree that, for the special purpose of the writer, the foreign term was the fitter:

(i) The immense superiority of the new French national spirit and organisation over the lifeless and old-fashioned machinery of the continental States of the *ancien régime* ensured the defeat of each successive Coalition. [*Ancien régime* is an admirable term to sum up conditions in France before the Revolution, conditions involving the concentration of power in the Court and the exploitation of the mass of the people to feed that power.]

(ii) He appointed an elaborate *rendez-vous* for the Brest and Toulon fleets in the West Indies. [*Rendez-vous* is the technical term for the assembly place of troops or ships. Perhaps we should not apply the term to less momentous meeting places.]

(iii) The speed of his *volte-face* bewildered and exasperated the British electorate. [*Volte-face* is the accepted term for a complete change in a person's attitude towards a political proposal.]

(iv) The *Daily Mail*, catering for the new half-educated democracy of all classes in a fashion quite different from that of the more solemn political organs which had satisfied the Victorian *bourgeoisie* .... [We could hardly dispense with this term for the shop-keeping middle class, with its respect for property and vested rights, and its suspicion of violent changes.]

There need be no heart searchings about most foreign importations. It is, indeed, a curious feature of English that we prefer the foreigner in other than the simple noun, verb, or adjective. There is the English *ear*; we go to Latin for *audible* (that can be heard), *auricular* (told in the ear, secret), *aural* (belonging to the ear), *aurist* (an ear specialist). English *sit* is replaced by its Latin cognate in *sedentary*; English *two* has as its corresponding noun *duplicity*, its corresponding adjective *dual* (from the Latin *duo*). English *foot* has *pedal* for its adjective and *pedestrian* as the equivalent of "foot-goer". The English pronoun *I* has the Latin *egoist* for the person always using *I*, the Latin *egotist* for the person always thinking about himself.

Full Stop (PERIOD). *Where should a Full Stop be placed?*

The "full-stop", or "period", indicates the close of a sentence, a sentence being a completely expressed thought. In a way the full-stop serves as a resting-place for a reader before he embarks upon the interpretation of another sentence; and modern usage, out of concern for the reader, provides these resting-places in plenty. Examine the instances in this little extract from Stevenson's *Will o' the Mill*:

One day, when Will was about sixteen, a fat young man arrived at sunset to pass the night. He was a contented-looking fellow, with a jolly eye, and carried a knapsack. While dinner was preparing, he sat in the arbour to read a book; but as soon as he had begun to observe Will, the book was laid aside; he was plainly one of those who prefer living people to people made of ink and paper.

The first sentences, you note, are quite short, each expressing one clear thought—the arrival of the young man, the descripton of the young man. The third, made up of clauses separated by semi-colons is much longer; and perhaps you might prefer a full-stop to a semi-colon after *aside*.

H (Unsounded, Mute). *In which words is the initial h without effect upon sound?*

A difficulty about the sounding or not sounding of *h* arises from the quite recent tendency to give a value to the letters by which a word is spelled. So it is that in several words, certainly without the *h* sound though with the *h* spelling a while ago, the *h* is now sounded. Thus "an humble, lowly, penitant and obedient heart" is the phrase; but we now rarely hear *humble* without the *h* sound. Sir Thomas Browne wrote, "For the World, I count it not an Inn but an Hospital, not a place to live but to die in"; but *hospital* now has with many the *h* sound.

In fact there are in modern English only about half a dozen words with mute *h*. We still write *an heir*, or *an heiress*, the *h* being silent. *Honour* ("Wear it for an honour in thy cap") and its derivatives ("He was descended from an honourable family"), *honest* ("He turns an honest penny"), and *hour* ("An hour they sat in Council") are other examples. We may perhaps anticipate, however, that *honour* and *honest* will not long remain without the *h* sound.

It may be well to note that in an unstressed syllable the *h* sound is hardly heard. Thus in "Hunt has scored his

third goal" neither *has* not *his* asks for more than the
tiniest *h* sound; and *forehead* still has the sound *forrid*.

Hackneyed Phrases. *What objection is there to the use of commonplaces?*

No very great objection exists. For their particular
purpose you could not better such phrases as these from
the Bible, "highways and hedges", "smote him hip and
thigh", "lick the dust", "a thorn in the flesh", "a broken
reed", "the root of all evil", "to be weighed and found
wanting", "a soft answer", "a word in season", "how are
the mighty fallen!" and a host of others that rush into
your mind. The plays of Shakespeare, too, have phrases
in plenty "familiar to our mouths as household words";
they may come pat to the purpose, and we have no sense
of indebtedness as we utter them. Nor is there any strong
reason why we should discard the use of phrases like
"sweets to the sweet", " 'Twas caviare to the general",
"metal more attractive", "life's fitful fever", and a
thousand more.

Yet we should be sparing in our use of these ready-
made phrases. For, torn from its content, the phrase may
lose its force; and it may have become so battered and
bruised with hard usage that it annoys our hearers or
our readers. Doesn't "the cup that cheers but not
inebriates" irritate you? Yet in Cowper's setting it is
delightful:

> Now stir the fire, and close the shutters fast,
> Let fall the curtains, wheel the sofa round,
> And, while the bubbling and loud-hissing urn
> Throws up a steamy column, and the cups,
> That cheer but not inebriate, wait on each,
> So let us welcome peaceful evening in.

Greatest danger of all, we may use the hackneyed phrase
in a quite inappropriate manner.

Thus, Shakespeare speaks of "cool reason"; and the
adjective is apt. For he is contrasting the boiling imagination of the lunatic (and of the lover) with the placid
mental processes of men in their senses:

> Lovers and madmen have such seething brains,
> Such shaping fantasies, that apprehend
> More than cool reason ever comprehends.

Now we may hear the adjunct *cool*—often *cold*—with *reason* whether called for or not: "the verdict of cool reason" is in general no more than "the verdict of reason".

"His or Her." *How do we manage to do without a Pronoun of the Common Gender?*

We are, lacking such a pronoun, torn between "correctness" that is stilted and an "incorrectness" that is easy. This sentence is an example of the first: "The passenger's luggage is carried at his or her own risk." This sentence of Shakespeare's is an example of the second: "God send every one their heart's desire."

The French language is a little better off than English in the matter. The French, like us, have nothing to represent "he or she"; but they have "son" to represent "his or her", and "soi" to represent "him or her". We are obliged to have makeshifts for all.

To be sure, when you are conscious that the correct is also the awkward, there is always the possibility of recasting your sentence. The colloquial expression, condemned by pedants, is "If every one minded their own business, the world would be a happier place". Correctness would have "If every one minded his or her own business". We get rid of both incorrectness and awkwardness by using the plural "If all of us minded our own business" or "If people minded their own business".

Further—and this is by law prescribed for interpreting Acts of Parliament—we are to take the masculine as including the feminine, *he* is equivalent to *he or her*. Some, apparently, resent this rule. Thus, the original version of a well-known hymn is "Soon will you and I be lying, Each within his narrow bed". The hymn-book version is "each within our narrow bed", a singular *each* with a plural *our*.

Homonyms (Homophones). *What are Homonyms?*

The Greek prefix *homo* signifies "the same": the word "homogeneous" for instance, means, "of the same kind". *Homonyms* are words alike in both spelling and sound: in "the bay horse", "the Bay of Biscay", "the bay window", "the bay tree" —— bay, one spelling and one sound, stands for four quite distinct words, different in origin and different in meaning. Words having the same sound with a variant in the spelling are at times called *Homophones*. Thus, in these three sentences we have *rays, raise, raze*, one in sound though distinct in spelling: "The sun whose rays are all ablaze with ever-living glory does not deny his majesty: He scorns to tell a story"; "I can raise no money by vile means"; "Canst thou not minister of a mind diseased, pluck from the memory a rooted sorrow, raze out the written troubles of the brain."

The presence in our language of so many homophones gives you a capital chance to test your power of distinguishing. For an instance, take *feign, fain, fane*. The first is *pretend* ("He escaped death by feigning death"); the second is the adjective *glad* ("I would fain die a dry death"); the third is the noun *temple* ("Iona's holy fane"). Can you distinguish one from another of the groups below?—bough, bow; guilt, gilt; skull, scull; cent, scent, sent; limb, limn; pray, prey; sword, soared; yolk, yoke; mean, mien; peak, pique; need, knead; vain, vein, vane; ware, wear; choler, collar; write, rite, right; through, threw.

Other languages have instances where the one sound (at times the one symbol) represents two quite distinct words. The very many instances in English have come largely through the simplifying of forms. Thus in *dough* (flour made into paste ready for baking) the now silent *gh* once stood for the *k* sound; loss of that sound made *dough* a homophone with *doe* (the female of the deer). The presence of so many invitations to ambiguity in English is something of a nuisance; and the nuisance is not wholly compensated by the many chances given of the mild form of humour called punning.

Idioms. *What is the explanation of a phrase like "I go to France next week"?*

Here we have an apparent clash between the present *I go* and the future *next week*; and this is an instance of those peculiarities in a language that we call *idioms*. The idiom often diverges from strict grammar: thus in "When I am dead, my dearest, sing no sad songs for me" *am*, the present form of the verb, clearly relates to the future. And usually we can give no very convincing reason for the idiom: we can only say that it is good English because custom has made it such. Analyse, for instance, an expression like "He'll do no more than he can help" and you find that in strictness it says the opposite of the interpretation you put upon it. "Than he cannot help doing" is called for by logic; yet the idiom persists and will persist. Compare the idiom that doubtless you have used many times, "I don't think it will rain", when you intend the meaning "I think it won't rain".

It is curious, and very interesting, that many of our common words have acquired idiomatic senses that diverge from the primary sense. The preposition *with* is a good example. The primary sense is "opposite to", "against"; and this the word retains in phrases like "contending with an enemy", "competing with a rival", "withstanding an onslaught". It was a natural development to apply the word from a physical to a mental attitude: "Be opposite with a kinsman, surly with servants", was the advice given to unlucky Malvolio.

And note these meanings: *accompaniment* ("She had a tongue with a tang"; "I'll do it with pleasure"), *means* ("He writes with a fountain-pen"), *in spite of* ("England with all thy faults I love thee still", "With the best intentions he failed"), *characterized by* ("The lady with the camellias"), *separation* ("I have parted with my best friend", "I can dispense with the money"), *in regard to* ("I can do nothing with him").

Impersonal Verbs. *How are Impersonal Verbs used?*

The verb in some sentences has no definite subject,

and we are obliged to supply the third person singular pronoun *it* as the subject. Thus: in "It never rains but it pours". You could not very well say for what noun the pronoun *it* stands—unless, indeed, you took refuge in the easy answer that "rain" is the noun ("The rain, it raineth every day"). One peculiar survival of the Old English impersonal is *methinks*. Here is Milton's: "Methinks I see in my mind a noble and puissant nation rousing herself like a strong man after sleep, and shaking her invincible locks. Methinks I see her as an eagle muing her mighty youth, and kindling her undazzled eyes at the full midday beam." *Thinks* there is different from *thinks* in "He thinks"; *methinks* is "it seems to me". So in Macbeth's outburst:

> Methought I heard a voice cry, "Sleep no more;
> Macbeth hath murdered sleep, the innocent sleep".

Methought is not "I thought" but "It seemed to me". You will not often wish to use the old form: better say "It seems to me" rather than "Methinks", and "It seemed to me" rather than "Methought".

Inflexions (also spelled "Inflections"). *Why do people call English an Uninflected Language?*

The adjective is not wholly justified. For we still have some inflexions. That is to say, we do make changes in some words in order to indicate changes in the meaning or in the application of the words: we add *s* to *ship* in order to denote the plural, we add *er* to *small* in order to denote the comparative degree of the adjective, we add *ed* to *walk* in order to denote the past tense of the verb. In the main, however, "uninflected" is applicable to English. Compared with Old English, with Latin and with some modern languages English has very few inflexions: our one adjective *beautiful* has to do duty for the French *beau*, *bel*, *belle*, *beaux*, and *belles*. We have hit upon more effective ways than inflexions of showing the modifications of words.

Thus, here is the Latin line, "Tendebantque manūs ripae ulterioris amore", a beautiful line you agree,—and this whether or not you know Latin. And it owes some of its beauty to the full sound of the word endings. We turn it into the English "And they were reaching forth their hands in longing for the farther shore". So turning it we have analysed inflexions into separate words—*tendebǎntque* has become *and they were reaching forth*, *ripae ulterioris* has become *of the farther shore*. Perhaps, in the process of replacing inflexions by words—prepositions mostly—some of the beauty of the language has gone. Musical vowels have gone and noisy consonants remain. Chaucer's line "And smalé foulés makén melodie" (where *smale*, *foules*, *maken* have each two syllables, and *melodie* four) becomes "And small fowls make melody". But the loss of beauty is more than made up by the benefit of simplicity.

Initials. *Is there any objection to the use of Initials instead of Complete Words?*

There can be no objection if you are quite certain that your hearer or your reader will be able to interpret the initials in the sense you intended. Courtesy, however, asks us not to put too heavy a burden upon our audience. "I am for a while O.P. to the B.O.F." comes from abroad; and the recipient of the letter is at a loss. We have now become so accustomed to speaking of "the B.B.C." that it is odd to hear "the British Broadcasting Corporation"; but we may well hesitate about using letters when more than one meaning can be attached to them or even when it needs an effort to expand them. In particular, we should be sparing in the use of letters for foreign words; for they are tricky at times, *i.e.* (the Latin *id est*), for instance, introduces an explanation, *e.g.* (the Latin *exempli gratia*) introduces an illustration, an example. The two are not always discriminated. These sentences illustrate the correct use: "We have words from two dialects of Old French; *e.g.* from Norman French come *catch*, *warden*, *launch*; from the dialect of Central France come their doublets *chase*, *guardian*, *lance*". "We can improve our writing by revision: *i.e.* we can make it more intelligible or more interesting or more persuasive."

Interjections (**Exclamations**). *What Punctuation Mark should be placed after Interjections?*

Usually the exclamation mark. Thus: "The wills above be done! but I would fain die a dry death"; "O! I have suffered with those that I saw suffer: a brave vessel who had, no doubt, some noble creatures in her, dashed all to pieces. O! the cry did knock against my very heart. Poor souls, they perished." "Good-night, good-night! parting is such sweet sorrow that I shall say good-night till it be morrow." This so even when the exclamation is in the form of a question. Look at this conversation between the irate Cleopatra and the Messenger:

C.: Is he married?
    I cannot hate thee worser than I do,
    If thou again say *Yes*.
M.: He is married, madam.
C.: The gods confound thee! dost thou hold there still!

Though the last five words are in the form of a question they are in fact an exclamation; and the exclamation mark not the question mark, rightly follows. So with: "The beauty of Israel is slain upon thy high places: how are the mighty fallen!"

Inversion. *Is it well to keep to the ordinary structure of an English sentence?*

Consider this: to write good English entails two tasks; you need to choose your words well; you need also to arrange those words in an effective order. The type of an English sentence is Subject followed by Predicate: thus "Sorrow and sighing shall flee away". There is some danger in departing from the type. For your readers, expecting it, may misinterpret the departure. Most of us, for example, fail to see at first that, in these lines of Gray's, the Subject is "inevitable hour" and that "the boast of heraldry" and so on goes with the Predicate as Object:

The boast of heraldry, the pomp of power,
    And all that beauty, all that wealth e'er gave,

> Awaits alike the inevitable hour:
> The paths of glory lead but to the grave.

By his unusual order—his inversion—Gray presented a puzzle.

But inversion does not always puzzle, and it may be very effective. The rule seems to be: keep to the normal order unless a good reason for departure exists. Thus, by putting a word or a phrase in an unexpected place, you draw attention to the word or phrase; you emphasize it. Look at these successful instances of inversion: "As cold waters to a thirsty soul, so is good news from a far country"; "Whatsoever thy hand findeth to do, do it with thy might" (Is not this more effective than "Do with thy might whatsoever . . . do"?); "Sweet are the uses of adversity".

Inversion seems almost called for in expressions of deep feeling. Look at the second half of Burke's sentence: "It is now sixteen or seventeen years since I saw the Queen of France, then the dauphiness, at Versailles; and surely never lighted on this orb, which she hardly seemed to touch, a more delightful vision." And in his later exclamation the inversion is in keeping: "Oh! what a revolution! and what a heart must I have to contemplate without emotion that elevation and that fall! Little did I dream . . . that she should ever be obliged to carry the sharp antidote against disgrace concealed in that bosom; little did I dream that I should have lived to see such disasters fallen upon her in a nation of gallant men, in a nation of men of honour and of cavaliers."

Inverted Commas. *When are Inverted Commas to be used?*

The inverted commas are appropriate to an exact quotation of a speaker's words or of an extract from another's writing. They are not appropriate in a report of what was said. Compare these:

> Doctor Johnson said, "Let me smile with the wise, and feed with the rich".

> Doctor Johnson's wish was that he should smile with the wise, and feed with the rich.

A quotation within the quotation is usually distinguished by having single, not double, commas. This from *Alice in Wonderland* illustrates:

"Do you mean that you think you can find out the answer to it?" said the March Hare.

"Exactly so," said Alice.

"Then you should say what you mean," the March Hare went on.

"I do," Alice hastily replied, "at least—at least I mean what I say—that's the same thing, you know."

"Not the same thing a bit!" said the Hatter. "Why, you might just as well say that 'I see what I eat' is the same as 'I eat what I see'."

[It will be noted that only the first commas marking off the quotation are inverted—turned upside-down. The commas closing the quotation are the ordinary ones though, like the first, raised above the line.]

Jargon. *What is meant by Jargon?*

Jargon is the term applied loosely—usually by people who dislike it—to pretentious language, to talk or to writing where there has been a determined effort to improve upon clear straightforward language. The hard-pressed reporter, anxious to fill up space and to lift his narrative out of the commonplace, may speak of "extinguishing a conflagration" when all he means is "putting out a fire", may expand "receive" into "be made the recipient of", "eat" into "partake of some refreshment", "portrait" into "counterfeit presentment", "house" into "domiciliary edifice". This is the journalistic jargon that journalists themselves laugh at. There is no particular harm in jargon; and we may get a great deal of fun from it: asked about a Government scheme that had been quietly shelved the Prime Minster said, "It has gone into innocuous desuetude"; and this was, for his purpose, more effective than "It has been forgotten". If you are fond of phrases like "the festive board", "the cup that cheers but not inebriates", "trip the light fantastic toe", don't discard them because a censor calls them jargon. But be sparing in the use of such: for most purposes it is better

to say "It is a long while since I saw you" than to copy
Mr. Micawber and say, "Years have elapsed since I had
an opportunity of ocularly perusing your lineaments".

Language as Vehicle of Thought. *Does language really carry thoughts from mind to mind?*

To embody thought so that another than the thinker
may share it is the great function of language. We must
recognize, however, that language is not a perfect means
of carriage, and that care on our part is requisite to make
it even tolerably good. The speaker puts his thought into
words; there is the first obstacle, the first cause of loss in
the transmission. For the speaker may be inept in his
choice of words or in his arrangement of them; and, when
all is said, a series of sounds is a very different thing from
a train of thought.

The second difficulty in the way of perfect transmission
is in the hearer, or reader. For in our use of language to
convey our thoughts we need another's co-operation; and
the needful co-operation may be a-wanting. The hearer
may be unable to co-operate. He may be ignorant of the
words we are using; or he may not have heard them
distinctly enough to recognize them; or he may attach to
them a meaning different from the one intended by us.
Or the hearer may be unwilling to co-operate with us.
He may not accede to our implied demand upon his
attention; and may not trouble to listen or to read. He
may even, out of sheer perversity, interpret our words in
an unintended sense.

That miscarriage and misunderstandings occur is a
fact. That fact imposes upon us a duty of care. Even in
speech we should give few occasions for misinterpretation;
and in writing, when deliberate consideration is possible,
the occasions should be rare indeed. Our dictionaries
(and our willingness to seek their aid) should preserve us
from at least one cause of misinterpretation; we need not
use words without an accurate knowledge of their meanings. For vagueness in our knowledge may easily mislead
us. Thus, "exceptional" and "exceptionable" are useful
words for two ideas, not one: the plan is exceptional when

it is out of the ordinary; the plan is exceptionable when it is faulty, when it is "open to exception". And notice these instances of words often confused with one another.

Chartered implies ownership of a charter conferring privileges; *charted* describes a sea of which the navigator has a chart.

Disinterested is impartial; *uninterested* is taking no interest in: a referee should be *disinterested* but not *uninterested* in the question set for his decision.

Recourse is a means of help to which one may resort; *resource* is a means of supplying help; it is foolish to have recourse to drink in order to fight trouble, a man of resource will find better ways.

Speciality is a thing in which a man specializes; *specialty* is the contract embodied in a deed.

Glance is a momentary look, *glimpse* is what we get by that look.

Contemptuous implies action showing contempt, *contemptible* implies deserving of contempt. [We have the wrong word in "I have a very contemptible opinion of you" and the right use in the retort, "I am not surprised; for all your opinions are contemptible".]

Deprecate is plead against, *depreciate* is belittle; we deprecate a proposed course of action, we depreciate the currency when we lessen its buying power.

Purpose is intend; *propose* is suggest; we purpose a journey when we intend to make it, we propose a plan when we put it forward for discussion.

Affect is modify; *effect* is bring about; close confinement will affect your health, but a holiday in the open air will quickly effect your recovery.

Complacent is pleased with oneself; *complaisant* is anxious to please others: the complacent man is quite contented, the complaisant man is obliging.

Compliment is praise, *complement* is a full muster: you compliment one upon his work, you obtain a complement when you get what is needed.

Illusion is deceit brought about by another; *delusion* is deceit brought about by yourself: you applaud the conjurer's illusions, but you are under no delusions about them.

Punctual is to the point in time; *punctilious* is to the point in honour; the punctual man observes the appointed time, the punctilious man "finds quarrel greatly in a strain when honour's at the stake".

Incredulous is reluctant to believe; *incredible* is hard to be believed: the first is active, the second passive. (Compare the pairs *intelligent* and *intelligible, appreciative* and *appreciable, curative* and *curable, ostentatious* and *ostensible*.)

Official is appertaining to an officer; *officious* is official to an unnecessary degree: a person is officious when he meddles more than he is called upon to do.

Length of Words. *Is it well to choose short words rather than long words?*

The answer to this qeustion depends upon the answers to these: Which words express the intended meaning with the greater effect? Which words will be the more readily interpreted in that intended meaning?

Nearly always the answer will be "the short words". When a choice presents itself choose, therefore, the short rather than the long. So doing you will be doing as the best writers do. Look at a passage or prose and one of poetry. The prose is from R. L. Stevenson's *Will o' The Mill*: "Up in Will's valley only the wind and seasons made an epoch; the fish hung in the swift stream, the birds circled overhead, the pine-tops rustled underneath the stars, the tall hills stood over all; and Will went to and fro, minding his wayside mill, until the snow began to thicken upon his head. His heart was young and vigorous; and if his pulses kept a sober time, they still beat strong and steady in his wrists. He carried a ruddy stain on either cheek, like a ripe apple; he stooped a little, but his step was still firm; and his sinewy hands were reached out to all men with a friendly pressure."

Examine this: you have 113 words. Of these four only —*overhead, underneath, vigorous, sinewy*—have more than two syllables; the first two are familiar compounds, the last two owe their third syllable to the adjective endings, *ous* and *y*. There are twenty-two disyllables, including the compound *pine-tops*. The rest, 87, are single syllables.

The poetry is Cleopatra's speech:

1. Give me my robe, put on my crown; I have
   Immortal longings in me; now no more
   The juice of Egypt's grape shall moist this lip.
   Yare, yare, good Iras; quick! Methinks I hear

5. Antony call; I see him rouse himself
   To praise my noble act; I hear him mock
   The luck of Caesar, which the gods give men
   To excuse their after wrath. Husband, I come:
   Now to that name my courage prove my title!

10. I am fire and air; my other elements
    I give to baser life. So; have you done?
    Come then, and take the last warmth of my lips.
    Farewell, kind Charmian; Iras long farewell.

Lines 1 and 12 are each ten words of one syllable; and (not counting the proper names) only lines 2, 8, 9, 10, 14 have two words with more than one syllable. And you agree that the short words are full of force. For one more instance look at Housman's *For the Fallen*:

Here dead lie we because we did not choose
   To live and shame the land from which we sprung.
Life, to be sure, is nothing much to lose;
   But young men think it is, and we were young.

Which of the pairs below, the first from the newspaper, the second a simpler alternative, is the more effective: "Lectures adapted to a juvenile auditory" (*Lectures suitable for boys and girls*); "The strike is bound to have disastrous repercussions" (*The strike is bound to have ill effects*); "It is difficult to believe that the responsible leaders of Labour and of Capital will not jeopardize a recovery which has brought them both so much benefit by plunging into a conflict from which neither is likely to derive any advantage compared with the inevitable sacrifices" (*Since the leaders know that so much will be lost and so little won, we think that there will be no strike*); "The Viceroy's speech made an excellent impression upon his audience" (*His hearers liked the Viceroy's speech.*)

It may be well to note, too, that when you do decide to use a long word, you should be quite certain of its meaning:

"And how long has your present vicar been here?"

"Mr. Mole, Sir, has been the incumbrance here, Sir, for nigh on forty years."

"Like" and "As" (COMPARISONS). *How are we to tell which word to use in Comparisons?*

Like is an adjective, peculiar in this that it takes the objective case after it. *Like*, therefore, is used when we compare things or persons. *As* is a conjunction; *as* is used, therefore, when we compare actions. Compare "He is like me" with "He does it as I do". Look at these examples of *like*: "All we like sheep have gone astray" (*like* compares erring people with straying sheep); "This is a hard world in winter for poor rogues like me"; "The barge she sat in, like a burnished throne, burned in the water" (*like* compares *barge* with *throne*). And here are examples of *as*: "As is the master, so is the man"; "She is as well as can be expected"; "Montigny leaped up, swift as an adder, and stabbed him to the heart".

Lucidity (Clearness). *What is Lucidity and how is it to be achieved?*

Lucidity is clearness: your speech or your writing has lucidity when an intelligent hearer or reader gets your intended meaning without great expense of time or thought. You have used plain words and have ordered them with effect; and so doing you have spared your hearer's or your reader's attention. You have not been vague (indefinite in thought or in expression) or obscure (hard to understand). In short, you have been good-mannered; for, say our neighbours, *clarté est politesse*—the courteous person tries to make you understand easily. This is how Cardinal Newman put it: "I may truly say that I have never been in the practice, since I was a boy, of attempting to write well, or to form an elegant style. I think I have never written for writing's sake, but my one and single desire and aim has been to do what is so difficult, namely, to explain clearly and exactly my meaning; this has been the whole principle of all my corrections and re-writings."

In Macaulay's Diary for January 12, 1850, is an interesting entry upon the matter:

> No doubt what I am writing will require much correction; but in the main I think it will do. How little the all-important art of making meaning pellucid is studied now! Hardly any popular writer, except myself, thinks of it. Many seem to aim at being obscure. Indeed, they may be right enough in one sense; for many readers give credit for profundity to whatever is obscure, and call all that is perspicuous, shallow. But *coraggio!* and think of A.D. 2850. Where will your Emerson be then? But Herodotus will still be read with delight. We must do our best to be read too.

Malapropism. *What is a Malapropism and how does it come about?*

A word, or an action, is *à propos* when it is pat to the purpose, when it is the very word or action that is most wanted; a word, or an action, is *mal à propos* when it is ill-fitted, awkward, ill-timed. And, so far as words are concerned, the awkwardness usually arises because of the wish to use long and imposing words: where these are used without precise knowledge of the meanings we have at times amusing results.

A character in Sheridan's play *The Rivals* is Mrs. Malaprop; and the ludicrous misuse of words is often called by her name. Here is her exposition of a scheme of education for her daughter:

> I would by no means wish a daughter of mine to be a progeny of learning. But I would send her, at nine years old, to a boarding school, in order to learn a little ingenuity and artifice. Then, sir, she would have a

supercilious knowledge in accounts;—and as she grew up I would have her instructed in geometry, that she might know something of the contagious countries;—but above all, Sir Antony, she should be mistress of orthodoxy, that she might not mis-spell and mis-pronounce words so shamefully as girls usually do; and likewise that she might reprehend the true meaning of what she is saying. This, Sir Antony, is what I would have a woman know:—and I don't think there is a superstitious article in it.

Perhaps you would consider what words should replace Mrs. Malaprop's *progeny, supercilious, geometry, contagious, orthodoxy, reprehend, superstitious* and others. But, of course, Mrs. Malaprop is not alone in misuse of words. Such misuse has existed since language began and will continue so long as people use words the meaning of which is not quite clear to them.

You blush when you realize that you have misused your language, when you have made a malapropism; but you get a deal of amusement out of the trips of others. You will perhaps rejoice in this letter that Miss Winifred Jenkins wrote to her friend in Wales. During her visit to London Winifred had "seen the park, and the paleass of Saint George's, and the king's and queen's magisterial pursing, and the sweet young princes, and the hillyfents, pyebald ass, and the rest of the royal family"; and she ends her letter with sound advice: "Dear Mary Jones! An' please God, when I return I'll bring you a new cap, with a turkey-shell coom, and a pyehouse sermon, that was preached in the Tabernacle; and I pray of all love, you will mind your writing and your spilling; for, craving your pardon, Molly, it made me suet to disseyffer your last scrabble, which was delivered by the hind at Bath. O, voman! voman! if thou hadst but the least consumption of what pleasure we scullers have, when we can cunster the crabbidot back off hand. . . . Remember me to Saul—poor sole it goes to my heart to think she don't know her letters. But all in God's good time. It shall go hard, but I will bring her the ABC in gingerbread; and that, you nose, will be learning to her taste. Mistress

says, we are going a long gurney to the North; but go
where we will, I shall ever be

Dear Mary Jones,

Yours with true infection,

London, June 3.   Win. Jenkins."

Metaphor. *Is it better to keep to the literal and banish the figurative from our writing?*

However much we strive to make our writing free from
adornment, we shall fail to keep the figurative—the
metaphorical as opposed to the literal—wholly out. We
cannot help transferring a name to something which it is
not in strictness applicable. Look at some of these transfers, these *metaphors* as they are called. In his *Ode to the
West Wind*, Shelley has the lines,

> I fall upon the thorns of life! I bleed!
> A heavy weight of hours has chained and bowed
> One too like thee—tameless, and swift, and proud.

You cannot overlook the transfers here. You know that
the trials and troubles in Shelley's life were not really
"thorns". They gave pain, true; but it was mental, not
physical pain: Shelley's "thorns" were not "stiff, sharp-
pointed woody processes on the stem of a plant".

But now look at these two lines from *Hamlet*: "To
what base uses we may return, Horatio." " 'Twere to
consider too curiously, to consider so." The word
consider does not straight away call into mind a vision of
something other than the intended meaning, "think
carefully". Hearing the word you do not see the astro-
loger surveying the stars and seeking from them reliable
conclusions. Yet *consider* is kin to *sidereal* (belonging to
the stars); it is a metaphor, though we are rarely conscious of that fact. *Examine* as a variant would be a
metaphor, too. *Examen* is the tongue of a balance:
"to examine you in Greek" is, strictly, "to weigh you in
the balance" and, very likely, find you wanting. The
implied comparison has been so often made, it is so
familiar to us, that in saying "examine" we are unaware

of our departure from the strictly literal sense. Much of our language is made up of such "dead" metaphors.

That is why it is rarely possible to define a word—*book*, for instance—in isolation. Having the context you may be able. The first meaning of *book* was wood of the beech-tree used as a writing tablet. But you say "This book weighs six ounces"; and then you have in mind the tangible thing, the leaves and the binding. The definition of *book* in that sense would seem to be something like, "A book is a collection of sheets, of paper or other material, fastened together to make a whole, and protected by covers". But this definition would not suit the context, "This book has been translated into many languages". Then it is that you are using *book* in Milton's sense when he speaks of a good book as "the product of a master spirit, preserved and treasured up on purpose to a life beyond life".

Farther from the first physical sense are "to be in his good books" (your name is in the record of those he delights to honour), "bringing him to book" (making him bring the authority for his statement), "speak like a book" (with such accuracy as the actual record has), "take a leaf out of his book" (follow his example).

So long as we don't strain after ornament there is no need to disdain metaphor. Mr. Churchill knows well how to use it:

> History with its flickering lamp stumbles along the trail of the past, trying to reconstruct its scenes, to revive its echoes, and kindle with pale gleams the passions of former days. What is the worth of all this? The only guide to a man is his conscience; the only shield to his memory is the rectitude and sincerity of his actions. It is very imprudent to walk through life without this shield, because we are so often mocked by the failure of our hopes and the upsetting of our calculations; but with this shield, however the fates may play, we march always in the ranks of honour.

Mixed Metaphor. *What is a "Mixed Metaphor"?*

The metaphors you employ—the implied comparisons

—may call into mind images that clash with one another. "Mixed metaphor" is the name sometimes given to this kind of ineptitude. We need not greatly worry when the metaphors have, by long and continual use, lost their first freshness, when they have become faded or "dead" metaphors. Thus, it seems to be over-scrupulous in finding fault with "Whether 'tis better to bear the slings and arrows of outrageous fortune, or to take arms against a sea of troubles". It is when the implied comparisons are vivid that a sense of incongruity may arise. The traditional example is: "Mr. Speaker, I smell a rat; I see him floating in the air and darkening the sky; but I'll nip him in the bud." The question of nightwear for the Forces was raised in Parliament, and *The Times* comment was: "Those aggressive pyjamas have won a *Blitzkreig*, and in the course of at most fifty years have swept the nightgown from the face of the civilized world."

Name-making (Onomatopœia). *What is meant by the expression "sound echoing sense"?*

The Greek word for "name-making" was onomatopœia. The word signifies the natural instinct to make a name (or a verb) by an imitation of the sound that we associate with the thing or the action. The sound creates its own name. Such "echo words" are *bang, cackle, fizz, gibber, giggle, hiss, mumble, pop, whirr, zip, flip, lisp,* and *ripple* ("The lisp of leaves and the ripple of rain").

The term is extended to the use of such words as by their sounds suggest the sense. Read aloud, for instance, Browning's lines and ask yourself whether they are suggestive of the galloping of horses:

I sprang to the stirrup, and Joris, and he;
I galloped, Dirck galloped, we galloped all three;
"Good speed!" cried the watch, as the gate bolts
   undrew;
"Speed!" echoed the wall to us galloping through.

Another capital illustration is from *The Ancient Mariner*. Note how the first four lines below are full of rush and movement, repeated *r*'s and *l*'s giving the ripple of water, repeated *f*'s suggesting the onrush of the ship. And note

how the contrasted long syllables in the last four lines
are suggestive of stagnation:

> The fair breeze blew, the white foam flew,
>   The furrow followed free;
> We were the first that ever burst
>   Into that silent Sea.
>
> Down dropt the breeze, the sails dropt down,
>   'Twas sad as sad could be;
> And we did speak only to break
>   The silence of the sea.

And here are four lines from Tennyson's *The Brook*:

> I chatter over stony ways
>   In little sharps and trebles;
> I bubble into eddying bays,
>   I babble on the pebbles.

Negatives. *What is the English idiom about Double Negatives?*

In our old literature to use two negatives together was
to make the negation more impressive; and, in much
colloquial talk, the multiple negative still aims at the
removal of all doubt about the negation. "I don't want
no more tea", you will hear, and even—if you go through
Covent Garden—something like "They'll not arf ask yer
no questions abaht it, but nothin' can't 'appen if yer act
as if yer never knowed nothin'—see?" And the hearer of
the advice is intended to interpret it as, "They'll ask you
a good many questions about it, but nothing can happen
if you act as if you knew nothing—see?"

The modern rule is: two negatives make an affirmative.
Say "I am not at all unwilling to help you", and your
hearer will understand you to say "I am very willing to
help you". The double negative makes the affirmative an
emphatic one. "A citizen of no mean city" is "A citizen
of a very great city". The judge is asked to decide that a
ship has been scuttled. He declines, "I am not merely not
satisfied that it has been done, but I am quite satisfied
that it has not".

Trouble may come in the use of words implying a

negative,—words like *deny* ("say that a thing is not true")
undeterred ("not deterred"), *under-estimate* "not value to
the full"), *discontinuous* ("not continuous"). Consider the
following:

   (i) You cannot deny that this tax will not be a burden
       upon industry.

  (ii) They were not in the least undeterred by their
       defeat from making another attempt.

 (iii) We cannot underestimate the effect of early
       education upon life.

  (iv) I heartily support the movement : no one yields
       to me in appreciation of its importance.

   (v) They represent value unequalled by few—and
       unsurpassed by none.

[In (i) *not* is superfluous; for *deny* already negatives.
In (ii) the *not* is again superfluous; for *un* in *undeterred* is
the negative prefix. In (iii) *under* should be *over*. In (iv)
no one is evidently meant to be interpreted as *every one*.
In (v) *unsurpassed* is *not surpassed*; and the advertiser
would have you think "surpassed by none".]

Nominative Absolute. *Is the Pronoun in an Absolute Phrase* I *or* Me?

The absolute phrase is usually regarded as taking the
nominative, *I, we, thou* and not the objective *me, us, thee.*
Look at these two lines from a sonnet of Shakespeare's:

    For summer and his pleasures wait on thee,
    And, thou away, the very birds are mute.

It is "thou" (not "thee"); the phrase is equivalent to an
adverbial sentence, "Because thou art away." A good
instance of the nominative absolute is this of Milton's:

    Then I shall be no more,
    And Adam, wedded to another Eve,
    Shall live with her enjoying, I extinct.

"I being extinct", that is.

You note that the absolute phrase is marked off by a
comma, or commas. Examples are: "My story being

done, she gave me for my pains a world of sighs"; "All that August night the fight continued, the stars rolling over in their majesty, but unseen through the sulphur clouds which hung over the scene."

Nominative Case. *When is a Noun or Pronoun in the Nominative Case?*

We have in modern English different pronouns for the nominative and for the objective cases: *I, we, thou, he, she, they,* for the nominative; *me, us, thee, him, her, them,* for the objective case. The subject of a sentence (that about which the statement is made) is in the nominative case: thus *I* is the subject of the several sentences in, "When I said I would die a bachelor, I did not think I should live till I were married".

It is important to remember, though, that some verbs join (or couple) another noun or pronoun to the subject rather than express doing. In the sentences "Tom grew a big boy" and "Tom grew potatoes", *boy* is clearly in the nominative, *potatoes* in the objective: you could invert the first with no loss of meaning, "A big boy grew Tom"; inversion of the second would be nonsense. So, "She became queen" and "The bonnet became her".

When the verb is a copulative verb, the following pronoun conforms to the case of the noun or pronoun preceding the copulative verb. Note these instances: "Alack, it was I who leaped at the sun" (*I* not *me*); "These are they which came out of great tribulation, and have washed their robes" (*they* not *them*); "Be of good cheer: it is I; be not afraid" (*I* not *me*).

It is in regard to our pronouns, which have one form for the nominative and another for the objective, that care is needed.

"None" (Pronoun). *Is the Pronoun "None" Singular or Plural?*

The answer to the question depends upon the meaning given to "none". *None* may be expanded into "no one" and then it is singular ("There is none like her, none", sings Tennyson). *None* may be expanded into "no persons", and then it is plural ("None of these, however, is known to us", writes Goldsmith). This latter it would seem is the more common expansion. Perhaps that is why Dryden's line, "None but the brave deserves the fair", is more often than not misquoted,—"deserve" the plural verb, taking the place of "deserves", the singular verb.

Though singular or plural may be justified, it is awkward to have both interpretations in the one sentence. Thus, this sentence needs a little adjustment: "With regard to the journalists asked to leave the country, the authorities point out that none of them has been ordered out because of their journalistic work." "None of them *has*" interprets *none* as singular; "*their* journalistic work" interprets *none* as plural. Better alter *has* into *have*; for *his or her*, as a variant of *their*, would be stilted.

Look at these instances: "If a due participation of office is a matter of right, how are vacancies to be obtained? Few die and none resign" (*None* is plural); "No one ever took him for a fool; but none, except his intimate friends, know he has a great deal of wit" (*None* is plural); "None does offend; none, I say, none". (*None* is singular).

Nouns, Verbs, Adjectives. *Which are the really important "parts of speech"?*

We arrange the words of our language in classes, assigning to each class words that do similar work. We may make the number of classes great or small; but we shall always place among the most important of our words these three kinds: (*a*) there will be names of things, (*b*) there will be words expressive of doing, (*c*) there will be describing words. That is, there will be Nouns, Verbs, Adjectives.

The first efforts of a child to signify its wants by means of speech are efforts to utter names. Long before the child can make the simplest statement (sentence, that is), he has at command a number of names. From his brief experience in the world he has learned to link together a sound with a thing; and he tries to articulate, to utter by means of his voice, the sound that brings to him what he wants—milk, or sugar, or toy, or mother. Much skill and a good deal of imagination is needed at the outset to interpret the immature utterances. Distinctness comes, though; and, by naming the things about him, the child has made the first great stride towards mastery of a language.

Names do not long content him. He acquires the ideas of actions; and *doing words* (verbs) are linked with the actions—*laugh, cry, walk, crawl.* Describing words—*pretty, sweet, sour, black, white*—come later.

The mother, very likely, will be able to interpret the child's words, uttered though they are without the joining words—the prepositions, conjunctions, relative pronouns—that show their relations. Thus, you find it difficult to extract a meaning from the words: "Alice came three-legged table, solid glass, tiny gold key, idea, doors, hall, locks too large, key too small, not open." You guess; but you are not sure. You are sure when the substantive words are fitly joined together:

> Suddenly Alice came upon a little three-legged table all made of solid glass; there was nothing on it but a tiny golden key, and Alice's first idea was that this might belong to one of the doors of the hall; but, alas! either the locks were too large, or the key was too small, but at any rate it would not open any of them.

"Number" of Nouns. *Is it always easy to know when a Noun is Singular or Plural?*

We need to know this in order to determine whether to use a singular or a plural verb. Usually it is quite easy to know; but a difficulty comes now and then. Strict grammar may be at war with logic; and then English idiom calls upon grammar to give way. In "The eight has been out this morning" *eight*, though a plural, is thought of as a unit: therefore it is that we have the singular verb *has*, and not the plural *have*. And in Pope's line, "Snuff or the fan supply each pause of chat," *snuff or the fan* is one thing at a time, a singular that is.

But *or* here joins rather than separates, and the verb *supply* is rightly in the plural.

Often we think of a number together as a unity. "He hit a six and a four" and "O, that we now had here but one ten thousand of these men in England that do no work to-day". We are so used to look upon the unity at times that the real plurality is in the background: we say "a fortnight" without thinking of "fourteen nights" and it sounds quite natural to say "The United States is the chief factor to be considered" (*is* not *are*).

Here lies the explanation of the idiom in such expressions as "Twice two makes four" (*makes* not *make*), "Three times six makes eighteen". (Those who use the singular verb look upon *two* or *six* as a single: "This group thrice repeated makes eighteen." Those who prefer *make*—and apparently there is no great difference between those that do and those that don't—regard *two* or *six* as a plural.

"Over-Stopping" (Punctuation). *Is there any objection to a great many Punctuation Marks?*

Consider the matter in this way. You punctuate your writing so as to afford some guidance to your hoped-for reader. By means of your various stops he will know how you intend your words to be grouped and also, at times, how you wish them to be read. But there is no need to be prodigal with your commas and full-stops. Your reader has intelligence, and you are entitled to expect him to exert it; perhaps you pay to that reader a pleasant compliment when you require much from him that he may reach your intended meaning. Not too much, you will understand; for he is unlikely to accede to great demands upon his attention. There may be under-stopping as well as over-stopping. But this latter, too, annoys; it is absurd to mark off every, even the slightest, pause in our sentences.

Look at *Alice's Adventures in Wonderland* for a pattern; your pleasure in reading the book is enhanced by the skilful punctuation, not excessive but enough. Here is a task—

Alice did not wish to offend the Dormouse again, so she began very cautiously: "But I don't understand. Where did they draw the treacle from?"

"You can draw water out of a water-well," said the Hatter; "so I should think you could draw treacle out of a treacle-well—eh, stupid?"

"But they were *in* the well," Alice said to the Dormouse, not choosing to notice this last remark.

"Of course they were," said the Dormouse; "—well in."

Here is a curious instance where over-stopping has distorted the sense. The fine old hymn that you sing to the tune of the "Old Hundredth" has the line,

> The Lord ye know is God indeed

and that is the correct way to write it. For the paraphrase of the line is "The Lord whom ye know is really God". That is, the line puts in emphatic manner the contrast between the gods of the heathen, "the work of men's hands", and the true God. In some editions the line is ruined by being printed

> The Lord, ye know, is God indeed.

To make "ye know" into a parenthesis is to present the hymn-writer as a gossip not quite sure of what he is saying.

Paragraphs. *What is the desirable length of a paragraph?*

The paragraph in some kinds of writing, in conversation pieces like the Alice passage above, will be very short, perhaps confined to a single line. In other kinds—a scientific exposition, a political or legal argument—the paragraph will be much longer. But the modern tendency is towards the short paragraph; and this tendency is probably a sensible one. You will keep your reader's attention the better by making your paragraphs fairly short—of not more than half a dozen or so sentences. The long paragraph is apt to find its reader mind-wandering before its end, just as the express train journey lulls us to sleep. The short paragraphs give repeated jerks to

attention, much as the stoppings of the slow train jerk
us away from the oncoming nap.

If we keep in mind what a paragraph should be, we
shall have no difficulty in deciding when to begin a new
one. A paragraph normally consists of a group of sentences explaining and supporting one another; it will be
either an introductory section, or a section connected
with but more or less distinct from the paragraphs before
and after. This example from Hazlitt's *On Going a
Journey* will illustrate. He has been explaining that in
general he dislikes talking while walking: the closing
words are:

> *At the sight of nature my fancy, poor as it is, droops
> and closes up its leaves, like flowers at sunset. I can make
> nothing out on the spot:—I must have time to collect
> myself.*

Then comes the paragraph in which he expands upon this
topic:

> *In general, a good thing spoils out of door prospects:
> it should be reserved for Table-talk. Lamb is for this
> reason, I take it, the worst company in the world out of
> doors; because he is the best within. I grant, there is one
> subject on which it is pleasant to talk on a journey; and
> that is, what one shall have for supper when we get to our
> inn at night. The open air improves this sort of conver-
> sation or friendly altercation by setting a keener edge on
> appetite. Every mile of the road heightens the flavour of
> the viands we expect at the end of it.*

In the last paragraph he takes up the topic of getting to
the inn for supper, and begins:

> *How fine it is to enter some old town . . .*

This of Macaulay's will serve as an instance of a well-
built paragraph: it is from his account of the trial of the
Bishops in James the Second's reign:

> The jury was sworn; it consisted of persons of highly
> respectable station. The foreman was Sir Roger
> Langley, a baronet of old and honourable family. With
> him were joined a knight and ten esquires, several of

c

whom are known to have been men of large possessions. There were some Nonconformists in the muster; for the Bishops had wisely resolved not to show any distrust of the Protestant Dissenters. One name excited considerable alarm, that of Michael Arnold. He was brewer to the palace; and it was apprehended that the government counted on his voice. The story goes that he complained bitterly of the position in whch he found himself. "Whatever I do," he said, "I am sure to be half ruined. If I say Not Guilty, I shall brew no more for the King; and if I say Guilty, I shall brew no more for anybody else."

Paraphrase. *Does Paraphrasing help towards a good English style?*

Paraphrasing—expressing the sense of a passage in words of your own—helps a great deal. Stevenson, indeed, ascribes his skill as a writer largely to the fact that he was a "sedulous ape", an eager imitator, of other writers. But, whether you set out to do it or not, you are in practice for ever paraphrasing. You paraphrase when you throw light upon an obscure passage, when you re-arrange a sentence so that no possibility of misinterpretation haunts it, when you smooth an unduly rough reply, when you make polite a brusque, churlish one. Consideration of your readers impels you to make changes whereby your writing becomes more readily intelligible, more forcible, more pleasing.

Mr. Micawber, after one of his poetic effusions, would at times be obliging enough as to paraphrase, turning the elaborate into the colloquial and simple:

"My other piece of advice, Copperfield, you know. Annual income twenty pounds, annual expenditure nineteen nineteen six, result happiness. Annual income twenty pounds, annual expenditure twenty pounds ought and six, result misery. The blossom is blighted, the leaf is withered, the god of day goes down on the dreary scene, and,—and, in short, you are for ever floored."

Much of our literature is successful paraphrase. Here, for instance, is a little of North's prose, itself derived from an earlier origin:

> And now for the person of her self: she was laid under a pavilion of cloth of gold of tissue, apparelled and attired like the goddess Venus, commonly drawn in picture: and hard by her, on either hand of her, pretty fair boys apparelled as painters do set forth God Cupid, with little fans in their hands with the which they fanned wind upon her.

And here is how Shakespeare ran the prose into verse:

> For her own person,
> It beggared all description; she did lie
> In her pavilion, cloth-of-gold of tissue,
> O'er-picturing that Venus where we see
> The fancy outwork nature: on each side her
> Stood pretty dimpled boys, like smiling Cupids,
> With divers-coloured fans, whose wind did seem
> To glow the delicate cheeks which they did cool,
> And what they undid did.

Parenthesis. *Is it well to break into a sentence with a Parenthesis?*

Certainly we should be sparing in our use of parentheses at any rate of long ones. The danger in the use comes from the fact that the insertion interrupts the even flow of our sentence; the reader is turned from the main statement and, before he reaches the end of the insertion, he may have lost the thread of that main statement. Still, the insertion of a word or a phrase or even another sentence, into a sentence for the purpose of modifying the statement made may be desirable. Consider some examples:

(a) In Lamb's sentence, *"Presents," I often say, "endear Absents"*, the place of "I often say", a parenthesis marked off by commas, is the natural place. So, too, in his sentence *An Oxford scholar, meeting a porter who was carrying a hare through the streets, accosts him with the extraordinary question:*

"*Prithee, friend, is that thine own hare, or a wig?*"
the parenthesis, *meeting . . . streets*, is in its fit
place.

(b) There can be no exception taken to the parentheses
below, marked off by brackets:

  (i) Go down to Kew in lilac-time, in lilac-time, in
      lilac-time;
      Go down to Kew in lilac time (it isn't far from
      London!)
      And you shall wander hand in hand with love in
      summer's wonderland;
      Go down to Kew in lilac-time (it isn't far from
      London!)   (*Alfred Noyes*)

  (ii) Lastly (and this is, perhaps, the golden rule), no
       woman should marry a teetotaller, or a man
       who does not smoke.   (*R. L. Stevenson*)

(c) Nor can one find fault with the parenthesis below,
marked off by dashes:
    A difference of colours in the stars—oftener read
    of than seen in England—was really perceptible
    here.

                                        (*T. Hardy*)

Passive Voice: Active Voice. *Is there any reason
  for using the Active Voice of the Verb rather than
  the Passive Voice?*

Consider the matter, and you will agree that the active
voice is better in one context, the passive in another. In
the sentence "Each horseman drew his battle blade",
horseman, the subject of the sentence, is the active agent,
and the verb *drew* is in the active voice, taking *battle blade*
as its object. We are laying stress upon the activity. In
the passive voice, however, we lay stress upon the result
of the activity. Thus, in the sentence "Men were driven
by want to desperate courses" the active agent is *want*;
the subject of the sentence, *men*, signifies the object of the
activity; and *were driven* is a verb in the passive voice.
The active form of the sentence—*Want drove men to*

desperate courses—shifts the emphasis from the passive sufferer to the active doer.

When we wish to make the sense of compulsion and suffering prominent, then the passive voice is fitting. This, for example, is Macaulay's account of the Jews:

> For centuries they have been outraged and oppressed banished from this place, imprisoned in that, deprived of their teeth, convicted of the most improbable crimes on the feeblest evidence, dragged at horses' tails, hanged, tortured, burned alive. When manners became milder, they have still been subject to debasing restrictions and exposed to vulgar insults, locked up in particular streets in some countries, pelted and ducked by the rabble in others, excluded everywhere from magistracies and honours.

When we wish to make the sense of vigorous action prominent, then the active voice is fitting. This example is from Tennyson's *Morte d'Arthur*:

> Sir King, I closed mine eyelids, lest the gems
> Should blind my purpose, for I never saw,
> Nor shall see, here or elsewhere, till I die,
> Not though I live three lives of mortal men,
> So great a miracle as yonder hilt.
> Then with both hands I flung him, wheeling him;
> But when I looked again, behold! an arm,
> Clothed in white samite, mystic, wonderful,
> That caught him by the belt, and brandished him
> Three times, and drew him under in the mere.

Personal Prounouns. *When is it desirable to use the Pronoun instead of the Noun?*

The pronoun gives scope for our indulging in the variety that pleases. By the use of *he*, *she*, *it* and the rest we avoid what may be disagreeable repetitions of a name. Look at these five sentences from Strachey's *Eminent Victorians*:

> The Miss Nightingale of fact was not as facile fancy painted her. She worked in another fashion, and

towards another end; she moved under the stress of an impetus which finds no place in the popular imagination. A Demon possessed her. Now demons, whatever else they may be, are full of interest. And so it happens that in the real Miss Nightingale there was more that was interesting than in the legendary one; there was also less than was agreeable.

Some might think that to replace *her* and *she*, wherever these personal pronouns occur, by *Miss Nightingale* would heighten the effect of the passage; most, however would dislike the substitution.

To be sure, since *he* may be *king* or *beggar*, *it* may be *dog* or *horse* or *book*, care in the use of the pronoun is called for. Our sentences should be so formed that no doubt arises about the noun for which the pronoun is a substitute. Note, too, that the pronoun is not invariably desirable though there is no doubt about its reference: "in the real Miss Nightingale" is better than "in the real her".

Personal Pronouns (Person). *What is meant by "Person" in Pronouns?*

Pronouns do more than enable us to avoid an unpleasing repetition; they enable us to determine whether the Person *speaks* or is *spoken to* or is *spoken of*. "I" (the First Personal Pronoun) stands for my name, and also identifies me with the speaker. *You* (the Second Personal Pronoun) identifies the person spoken to. *He* (the Third Personal Pronoun) identifies the person spoken of. Usually there are corresponding distinctions in verbs: *I am; Thou art; He is*, and so on. Two points are worth noting when you use the personal pronouns. The first is that a narrative in the First and Second Persons i. more vivid, more dramatic, than one in the Third Person. Thus, in North's *Plutarch*, you have a narrative in the Third Person:

Taking Caesar's gown all bloody in his hand, he laid it open to the sight of them all, showing what a number of cuts and holes it had upon it.

Shakespeare dramatizes this in the **First and Second** Persons:

> If you have tears, prepare to shed them now,
> You all do know this mantle: I remember
> The first time ever Caesar put it on;
> 'Twas on a summer's evening, in his tent,
> That day he overcame the Nervii:
> Look! in this place ran Cassius' dagger through:
> See what a rent the envious Casca made;
> Through this the well-beloved Brutus stabb'd.

The second point is this: the English idiom, when a First Personal Pronoun and another are together, is to postpone the First Personal Pronoun. It is "You and I are aware" (not "I and you"), "He and I were there" (not "I and he"). This is different from the idiom of Latin, which gives precedence to the First Person: it is *Ego et tu* (I and thou).

On occasions—which probably should be rare—one prefers to write in the Third Person. Thus, "Mrs. A. presents her compliments to Mrs. B. and regrets that she is unable to recommend as nursemaid the girl about whom Mrs. B. inquires".

Personification. *When we personify a lifeless thing shall we make the corresponding Pronoun Masculine or Feminine?*

You personify when you make an imaginary person represent an abstract idea or an intangible thing. In "She sat like Patience on a monument smiling at grief" Patience is an instance of personification, as Honour and Freedom are in these lines of Collins:

> By fairy hands their knell is rung,
> By forms unseen their dirge is sung.
> There Honour comes a pilgrim grey
> To bless the turf that wraps their clay,
> And Freedom shall awhile repair
> To dwell, a weeping hermit, there.

You note, by the way, that you write the personification with a capital. When we thus endow lifeless things with life and feeling, it is in great measure a matter of taste whether to regard them as men or as women. Words-worth, thinking of the beauty and the cheering nature of *Hope*, makes it feminine, *her* and *she* being the corre-sponding pronouns:

> Hope rules a land for ever green;
> The powers that serve the bright-haired Queen
>   Are confident and gay:
> Clouds at her bidding disappear;
> Points she to aught, the bliss draws near
>   And Fancy smooths the way.

Its characteristics being turbulence and uncouthness, Collins makes *Anger* masculine:

> Next, Anger rushed, his eyes on fire,
>   In lightnings owned his secret stings;
> In one rude crash he struck the lyre
>   And swept with hurried hand the strings.

Cowper, thinking—quite erroneously—that *Knowledge* and *Wisdom* are attributes peculiar to men, makes these attributes masculine:

> Knowledge is proud that he has learned so much,
> Wisdom is humble that he knows no more.

Place of Preposition. *Is it a fault to have the Preposition after its Noun or Pronoun?*

The word preposition itself suggests that the natural (and therefore usual) place is before the noun or pronoun in the objective case; and this is what we usually find. "They that sow in tears shall reap in joy": obviously the place for *in* is before *tears* and before *joy*. So in the sen-tence, "I grew weary of the sea, and intended to stay at home with my wife and family", the prepositions—in the phrases of *the sea*, *at home*, *with my wife*—precede the noun.

Yet it is good English idiom on occasion to have the preposition after the noun or pronoun, and even at the end of a sentence. We do, in fact, say "The people I was travelling with" and not "the people with whom I was travelling", "the book I found it in" and not "the book in which I found it"; and no schoolboy would say "For what are you hitting me?" The curiosity is that, when we take pen in hand we often think proper to desert the good idiom of speech.

At times we can hardly avoid the end preposition. We cannot when the defining relative *that* is used: "Better bear those ills we have than fly to others that we know not of." And when the interrogative pronoun occurs, it is more comfortable to have the preposition later in the sentence. "What do you take me for?" comes trippingly to the tongue; you could hardly express the same intended indignation by "For what do you take me?"

Plural (Abbreviations). *How is the Plural of Abbreviations indicated?*

When the abbreviation has become a recognized word, the plural is indicated in the usual way: *wig* (short for *periwig*) has the plural *wigs*, *curio* (short for *curiosity*) has the plural *curios*. When the abbreviation consists of letters, the plural is indicated by a doubling of the last letter. Thus the plural of *MS.* (*manuscript*, that is) is *MSS*. *LL.D.* is for *Doctor of Laws*, *Britt.* on our coins is the plural of *Britains*.

Plural Nouns (Spelling of). *What are the rules about the Spelling of Nouns in the Plural?*

Usually an *s* or an *es* is added to the singular in order to indicate the plural: *town* becomes *towns*; *soldier*, *soldiers*; *year*, *years*; *tress*, *tresses*; *church*, *churches*. The spelling of the plurals, below, however, needs careful notice:

(1) In such a word as *calf* the *f* is modified by the *s* sound of the plural and becomes a *v* sound: *calf* becomes *calves*; *knife*, *knives*; *loaf*, *loaves*; *sheaf*,

sheaves. But some words keep the *f* sound un-modified by the *s* sound; *chiefs, briefs, roofs, fifes* (the musical instruments, that is, *fives* having a different meaning), *hoofs* (but Tennyson has *hooves*: "His broad clear brow in sunlight glowed; on burnished hooves his war-horse trode").

(2) The single vowel *y* unites with the *e* of the plural ending to make *ie*: *lady* becomes *ladies; ruby, rubies; soliloquy, soliloquies* (the *u* here going with *q* to make the *kw* sound and the *y* remaining a single vowel).

In words like *key, toy, bay,* the *y* forms part of a diphthong, or double vowel, and it remains in the plural: *keys, donkeys* (contrast with *ponies*), *days.*

(3) There are in modern English some survivals of old plurals and some recent importations that still cling to their foreign endings. Thus, *men, women, feet, mice, children, oxen,* all bear trace of their Old English origin. The Latin singular *radius* becomes in the plural *radii; maximum* becomes *maxima,* though *maximums* is encroaching; *stratum* becomes *strata; species* remains unaltered for the plural; *thesis* becomes *theses; basis* becomes *bases; opus* becomes *opera.* The Greek singular *ellipsis* becomes in the plural *ellipses, analysis* becomes *analyses, parenthesis* becomes *parentheses, phenomenon* becomes *phenomena.* [But Dickens knew the instinct of the language and wrote, "Mr. and Mrs. Crummles who have bought up a talented and virtuous family to be blessings and phenomenons".] We have the French plurals *beaux* and *messieurs* (of which the abbreviation "Messrs." serves as our plural of "Mr."): we have the Italian *banditti* (but *bandits* is the more common form), and *libretti;* and we have the Hebrew *cherubim* and *seraphim* (but *cherubs* and *seraphs* are the usual forms).

(4) Some curious plurals are these:

Stigmata as plural of *stigma,* a Greek word meaning mark or sign; but *stimas* is found. *Irides* as plural of *iris,* meaning "an appearance like the rainbow" but we have *irises* too: the adjective is *iridescent* (gaily coloured).

Miasmata as plural of *miasma* ("infectious and polluting matter in the air"), but *miasmas* also serves as plural.

Dilettanti as plural of *dilettante*, an Italian word signifying one that dabbles in art, that loves painting or music but gives no serious study to them.

Genera as plural of *genus*, a Latin word signifying a group of similar things that may again be divided into smaller groups called *species*.

Corps used for both singular and plural. In writing there is no means of distinguishing singular from plural; but in speaking the singular is *kor*, the plural is *kors*.

Hiatus (pronounced $h\bar{i}\text{-}\bar{a}t\text{-}\bar{u}s$, i.e. all the vowels long) as plural of *hiatus*, the *u* vowel being short; but *hiatuses* also occurs. The word is applied to a succession of two vowels with no intervening consonant, as in "no others"; it is also applied to a gap in a series.

Octopodes as plural of *octopus*, a Greek word signifying eight-armed (or -legged); but we may expect *octopuses* to prevail over the foreigner.

Plurals (Compound Words). *What are the rules for the Plurals of Compound Nouns?*

In general, when a noun is composed of two or more elements, the plural sign appears on the last element only: thus *girl clerks, boy messengers, bookcases, coach-houses, apple trees.* But there are sentences where both elements take the plural sign; and this appears to be invariably so when *man* or *woman* is the first element: thus *men-servants* and *women-servants* (but *maid-servants*).

When the compound noun—as in *letter-patent, court-martial, knight-errant, heir apparent, attorney-general, account-current*—consists of a noun and its attendant adjective, the general rule is to place the plural sign with

the noun only, *letters-patent, courts-martial, knights-errant,*
and so on. When, however, the two words are so closely
knit that they make one word, the plural sign comes at
the end: *court-martials* is, for instance, the ordinary plural
though in formal writing *courts-martial* persists. Notice
the difference between *hand full* and *handful*: we write
"She came with her hands full of flour" but "She uses
two handfuls of flour for her pancakes".

Plurals (Courtesy Titles). *What are the rules for the Plurals of Names and Titles?*

The ordinary plurals of proper nouns present no
difficulty: "We must keep up with the Joneses", "Shall
we ask the Robinsons to the wedding?" But how are we
to indicate that we refer to more than one Mr. Brown,
more than one Mrs. Brown, more than one Miss Brown?
Modern English has evolved some curious answers.

The natural plural for *Mr.—Misters* is confined to talk,
talk intended to be jocular, and to the writing representing such talk. It is not found in literary English. For
formal and commercial language we go to France to seek
a plural: we write *Messrs.*, the abbreviated form of
Messieurs (plural of *Monsieur*).

Mrs. with the *s* ending raises a problem. We can hardly
say *Missesses*: our instinct to prefer easy instead of
difficult sounds impels us to transfer the plural sign to the
second element and say, as well as write, "the two Mrs.
Browns", or even allow the plural to appear from "two"
and write "the two Mrs. Brown".

The plural *Misses* is easy enough to pronounce, and in
formal writing and speech this plural is customary. You
would invite the "Misses Brown" and so name them in
the list of guests. Ordinarily, however, you say and write
"The Miss Browns". There seems, for instance, to be a
distinction between "the Miss Inderwicks, as the girls
called them, and the Misses Inderwick, as they called
themselves".

You will note that the title of a book or a play, though
in the plural form, takes the verb in the singular: "The
Newcomes was written by Thackeray."

Pronunciation. *Is it possible to be certain about the pronunciation of English words?*

If we observe carefully and imitate the speech of cultured people, we shall go far towards certainty; but we can never be quite certain. For uniformity does not exist. This is how Webster's *New International Dictionary* puts it: "The standard of English pronunciation, so far as a standard may be said to exist, is the usage that now prevails among the educated and cultured people to whom the language is vernacular; but, since somewhat different pronunciations are used by the cultivated in different regions too large to be ignored, we must frankly admit the fact that, at present, uniformity of pronunciation is not to be found throughout the English-speaking world". Thus, the "best speakers" in America make *leisure* rhyme with *seizure*, the "best speakers" in Britain with *pleasure*. In *either* and *neither*, though many still keep the long *e* sound, the majority make *ei* equivalent to long *i*. This long *i* has, indeed, a capacity for displacing other vowels. In London and its environs it even encroaches on the long *a* in words like *cake, hate, pain*.

A few words about the pronunciation of which doubts may arise are these:

dishevel (*di-shév-el*): *shevel* is for the Old French *chevel* meaning *hair* and the prefix is *di* not *dis*;

laboratory (*láb-or-a-tory*) the abbreviation *lab.* may tend to keep the accent on the first syllable; but *lab-ór-at-or-y* is more comfortable and will probably prevail;

apparátus (plural *apparatuses*): the accent is on the third syllable, and *átus* rhymes with *mate us*;

decadent: the accent is on the first syllable and the first *e* like the last is short;

vagáry (a freak): the accent is on the second syllable, and the word rhymes with *wary*;

déspicable: the accent is on the first syllable, and the vowels are all short;

súbsidence: the *i* is short as in *residence, confidence, coincidence*, though the *i* remains long in *subside*;

éxigency: accent on the first syllable and short *i*;

ad-vér-tise-ment (accent on the second syllable) but *ád-ver-tise;*

aged, meaning "having lived long", "very old", is *a-jed* (long *a*), in a phrase like "aged twelve" the word is *ajd* (only one syllable);

aye, meaning "yes" as in "The Ayes have it" rhymes with *eye,* meaning "ever" as in "For ever and aye" it rhymes with *may;*

bow, meaning a curve or something shaped in a curve (*rainbow, bow and arrow, bow window*), rhymes with *go,* meaning an inclining of the head it rhymes with *low.*

cinema (sin-em-a: in spite of the allied word *ki-net-ic,* with the long *i* and the accent on the second syllable, the pronunciation given will prevail);

clematis (clém-á-tis, accent on the first syllable and long *a* sound);

communal (com-mūn-al, accent on the second syllable and long *u* sound);

conjure (in the sense, *juggle,* "The speaker conjured up a delightful vision", the pronunciation is *kun-jer;* in the sense, *solemnly appeal,* "I conjure you to pause before you decide, the pronunciation is *kon-jóor*).

extempore (ex-tem-por-e, four syllables);

finale (fin-ah-li, long *i* and accent on the second syllable);

glacier (glá-ci-er, short *a* and accent on the first syllable);

vagary (vag-á-ri, long *a* for the accented second syllable).

Proper Nouns becoming Common Nouns. *In what way does the name of a person become applicable to other persons or places?*

A Proper Noun is, strictly speaking, an index only: it has no meaning, no connotation we say; it indicates, denotes, the one particular person or place. But that person or place may become well known for some reason or other; people hearing the name will call to mind the reason. The name thereby acquires connotation. The person or place becomes a type and the name is applied to persons or things that may be classed with that type. "Some mute, inglorious Milton here may rest", writes Gray; one, that is, endowed with the poet's nature and capacity but starved because "Knowledge to his eyes her ample page, Rich with the spirits of time did ne'er unroll". "A Daniel come to judgment! yea, a Daniel", exclaims Shylock, using the proper name to signify what Daniel was, a wise, just judge.

A further development is when from the proper noun a descriptive adjective has been evolved. Atlas was the god that held up the pillars of the universe, he bequeathed his name to the Libyan mountains; he also bequeathed to us the adjective *Atlantean*:

> Sage he stood,
> With Atlantean shoulders, fit to bear
> The weight of mightiest monarchies.

Thus, Stentor, the loudest shouter among the warriors that fought before Troy, has left us *stentorian*. Hercules, the type of formidable strength able to overcome whatever obstacles, has left us the adjective *herculean*: "a herculean task" is one that calls for our utmost powers.

Propriety (Fitness) of Expression. *What considerations should guide in the choice of words?*

Your own taste will very likely be your best guide. You have a topic and you anticipate an audience; you will therefore select words suited to topic and to audience. Thus, having consideration for your audience, you will prefer the simple expression to the difficult; you will say "He was fond of fishing" rather than "He was an ardent devotee of the piscatorial art". You will think the words of the *Proverbs* more effective than those of Dr. Samuel Johnson. The *Proverbs* enjoin: "Go to the Ant, thou Sluggard, consider her ways, and be wise: which having no guide, overseer, or ruler, provideth her meat in summer, and gathereth her food in the harvest. How long wilt thou sleep O sluggard? When wilt thou arise out of thy sleep? Yet a little sleep, a little slumber, a little folding of the hands to sleep. So shall thy poverty come as one that travelleth, and thy want as an armed man."

Does anyone prefer Doctor Johnson?:—

> Turn on the prudent "Ant" thy heedless eyes,
> Observe her labours, Sluggard, and be wise;
> No stern command, no monitory voice,
> Prescribes her duties, or directs her choice;
> Yet, timely provident, she hastes away
> To snatch the blessings of a plenteous day;
> When fruitful Summer loads the teeming plain,
> She crops the harvest, and she stores the grain.
> How long shall sloth usurp thy useless hours
> Unnerve they vigour, and enchain thy powers?
> While artful shades thy downy couch enclose,
> And soft solicitation courts repose,
> Amidst the drowsy charms of dull delight,
> Year chases year with unremitted flight,
> Till Want now following, fraudulent and slow,
> Shall spring to seize thee, like an ambushed foe.

Under propriety—fitness of expression—comes also accordance with recognized usage. For instance, here are the opening lines of Shelley's sonnet:

> I met a traveller from an antique land,
> Who said "Two vast and trunkless legs of stone".

Are these "the two first lines" or "the first two lines"? Clearly, the second; we should need two sonnets to have "two first lines".

Or consider the sentence "I like . . . kind of books": is the adjective before *kind* to be *this* or *these*. Clearly, since *kind* is singular we need *this*; yet how often we find *these*. And wouldn't fitness of expression call on you to modify the sentences below?—

(a) Each of the ladies, like two excellent actresses, were perfect in their parts. [Each . . . was . . . in her part.]

(b) Being a plain and straightforward man, the proposal strikes me as dishonest. [Re-arrange the sentence, and the awkwardness goes: The proposal strikes me, being a plain and straightforward man, as dishonest.]

(c) I doubt I will not pass the examination. [I fear that I shall not pass the examination.]

(d) You and I are both agreed upon these sort of questions. [Either *this sort of question* or *these sorts of questions.*]

(e) The magistrate said that he would endeavour to administer justice without leaning either to partiality on the one hand or to impartiality on the other. [The flood of words has betrayed the speaker into a contradiction of himself. Write simply "to administer justice impartially".]

(f) He only wrote on one side of the paper. [Probably the intended sense is "He wrote on one side only of the paper".]

(g) Why, her and me were the best of friends before him and her met. Of course this is between you and I. [This abuse of the pronoun is a little exaggerated in the extract. Better say "Why, she and I . . . before he and she met . . . between you and me".]

(h) The new Spring styles are so varied that no one can fail to obtain a hat that will not suit them. [Write "that will suit her".]

(i) That moiety of the population wont to be termed the gentler sex has created much stir of late. [Better translate the circumlocution into "women", and write "Women have created much stir of late".]

Prose. *What is the chief distinction between Prose and Verse?*

Prose is straightforward speech in which there is no regular recurrence of unaccented and accented syllables. Verse is speech arranged in regular groups of unaccented and accented syllables. In the writing of prose the lines are as long as the paper will bear; in writing verse there is a turning back to the beginning when each set of regular groups is ended.

Contrast these few sentences of capital prose with the

lines of verse that follow. Here is the prose: "It is almost a definition of a gentleman, to say he is one who never inflicts pain. This description is both refined and, so far as it goes, accurate. He is mainly occupied in merely removing the obstacles which hinder the free and unembarrassed action of those about him; and he concurs with their movements rather than take the initiative himself. His benefits may be considered as parallel to what are called comforts or conveniences in arrangements of a personal nature; like an easy chair or a good fire, which do their part in dispelling cold and fatigue, though nature provides both means of rest and animal heat without them."

You notice that the accents in the passage have no regular sequence; they are not like the recurring strong and weak notes in a bar of music. But now read aloud these four lines of Pope:

A little learning is a dangerous thing:
Drink deep, or taste not the Pierian spring:
There shallow draughts intoxicate the brain,
But drinking largely sobers us again.

You notice the regular beat of weak accent followed by strong accent.

Perhaps it is well to add that, though we use the adjective *prosy* in the sense "dull and wearisome", good prose is by no means distasteful. There are glorious passages of prose as of verse. This bit of Hamlet's prose, for example, gives much the same kind of thrill as his verse soliloquy does:

I have of late—but wherefore I know not—lost all my mirth, forgone all custom of exercise; and indeed it goes so heavily with my disposition that this goodly frame, the Earth, seems to me a sterile Promontory; this most excellent Canopy, the Air, look you, this brave o'erhanging Firmament, this Majestical Roof fretted with golden fire, why, it appears no other thing to me than a foul and pestilent congregation of vapours. What a piece of work is a man! How noble in Reason! how infinite in faculty! in form and moving, how express and admirable! in Action how like an Angel! in apprehension how like a God! the beauty of the world! the Paragon of Animals! And yet, to me, what is this Quintessence of Dust? Man delights not me.

Punctuation (Purpose of). *What is the object of Punctuation?*

We punctuate—we insert "points" or "stops"—in order to help our readers towards the correct interpretation of what is written or printed. The stops, for one thing, indicate how the words are to be grouped. Thus, in the carol, "God rest you merry, gentlemen", the comma after "merry" preserves you from the misreading frequent with carol-singers: the line is not the quite meaningless "God rest you, merry gentlemen".

The stops also help, but this is their subsidiary duty, to indicate the tone in which the writer would like his words to be uttered. Thus, Macbeth suggests to his wife that their plot might fail: "If we should fail," he says. Lady Macbeth rejoins "We fail". One actress, interpreting this as a scornful dismissal of the suggestion, would have the exclamation mark "We fail!" and would emphasize both *we* and *fail*. Another actress, and perhaps preferably, would interpret the words as a grim acceptance of the results of failure and would have the period "We fail". The antithesis following comes then with the greater effect "But set your courage to the sticking-point, and we'll not fail".

The stops are the substitutes in writing or printing for the pauses, the voice changes, the gestures that aid interpretation in speech. The sentence below, for instance, is readily grasped when heard; but, being written, it clamours for indication of how its words are to be grouped:

Unquestionably as a general proposition when an offer is made it is necessary in order to make a binding contract not only that it should be accepted but that the acceptance should be notified.

A little patience will, it is true, enable us to determine the matter; but the stops are welcome:

Unquestionably, as a general proposition, when an offer is made, it is necessary, in order to make a binding contract, not only that it should be accepted, but that the acceptance should be notified.

And the little dialogue below illustrates how stops may indicate tone and alter meanings: the last three words will be interpreted by you in three differing ways:

"How do I get to the Strand?" "Turn to the right." "Right?" "Right." "Right!"

Quotations. *Does it help to introduce Quotations into one's speech or writing?*

Whether or not you are conscious of it you are for ever quoting; and there is not the least reason why you should not. When the quotation is apt, and when it brings into your reader's mind pleasant memories, it becomes a great delight. Besides, your quotation may be so much a part of everyday language that you do not recognize it as a quotation.

These phrases from the Bible, for instance, are often used without a realization that they are extracts,—perhaps more often than not: "the apple of his eye", "the stars in their courses [fought against Sisera]", "bring down my grey hairs with sorrow to the grave", "entreat me not to leave thee", "to cast pearls before swine", "the eleventh hour", "hoping against hope", "a howling wilderness", "a labour of love", "a perfect babel", "a painted Jezebel", "the shibboleth of his party". And you very likely use these phrases from Shakespeare without any clear idea of where you found them, "familiar in their mouths as household words", "a tale told by an idiot, full of sound and fury", "a Daniel come to judgment", "the harmless, necessary cat", "such stuff as dreams are made on". Why, a single speech of Hamlet's supplies us with a score of phrases that have become a real part of the language, phrases constantly used by people quite unaware that they are quoting. Look at a few lines of the speech, and ask yourself how often you have heard phrases from it:

To be or not to be—that is the question;—
Whether 'tis nobler in the mind to suffer
The slings and arrows of outrageous fortune,
Or to take arms against a sea of troubles,
And by opposing end them?—To die,—to sleep,—
No more; and by a sleep to say we end
The heart-ache and the thousand natural shocks
That flesh is heir to,—'tis a consummation—
Devoutly to be wished. To die,—to sleep,—
To sleep—perchance to dream—ay, there's the rub.

"To be or not to be", "there's the rub", "a consummation devoutly to be wished", "flesh is heir to",—the phrases are as current as coppers.

There is a danger about quotations: those unfamiliar with the quotation may resent it. They may think it to be introduced rather to display the writer's knowledge than to inform the reader's ignorance. This is especially so when the quotation is in another language. Bahram's reader familiar with Latin, for instance, delights in the lines:

> *Eheu fugaces*
> What Horace says is—
> *Eheu fugaces*
> *Anni labuntur, Postume, Postume!*
> [Years glide away, and are lost to me, lost to me!]

The reader unfamiliar with Latin will not delight in them.

Quotation Marks (Single or Double Commas.)
How do you mark off a Quotation within a Quotation?

You get the answer to this question by examining an instance. Take this from *Alice in Wonderland*:

"You should say what you mean," the March Hare went on.

"I do," Alice hastily replied, "at least—at least I mean what I say—that's the same thing, you know."

"Not the same thing a bit!" said the Hatter. "Why, you might just as well say that 'I see what I eat' is the same as 'I eat what I see'!"

The interior quotations "I see what I eat" and "I eat what I see", being interior and not as in this present sentence, are marked off by single commas (or quotes). And notice the gathering of stops at the end of the sentence—the single raised comma to show the end of the interior quotation, the exclamation mark to indicate the tone of scorn, the double raised commas to indicate the close of the main quotation.

Such is the usual method. But you will come across writers (or their printers) that prefer the single commas for the main quotation, reserving the double ones for a possible internal quotation. Perhaps this is the more logical. But, after all, the internal quotation is rare; and doubling the commas does make the quotation more conspicuous.

We sometimes speak of these quotation marks as "inverted commas". But you will notice that it is only the commas at the beginning of the quotation that are inverted—turned upside down, that is. Those at the end are the ordinary commas raised above the line.

Relative Pronoun. *Are there means of deciding when to use "Who" or "Whom" or "That"?*

It is in reference to these pronouns that errors in English grammar most often occur. Maybe, indeed, we should not call them "errors" but merely departures from what is taught in class and in the grammar text-book. The errors come in the main from the fact that the pronouns ("relative pronouns" they are called) fulfil two functions: they are noun-substitutes; they also act as joining words, as conjunctions. Consider a few examples. First, look at examples where the relative pronoun introduces what you might call a defining clause. In "This is the house that Jack built", the clause "that Jack built" defines "house"; and the appropriate relative is *that*, whether it is the subject or (as here) the object of its own clause. In the lines "He that shall live this day, and see old age, will yearly on the vigil feast his neighbours" *that*, the defining relative, is the subject—the nominative case—in its own clause. Other instances of the defining relative are:

"Who is this that darkeneth counsel by words without knowledge?" (*Who* here is the interrogative pronoun, not the relative); "He that is slow to anger is better than the mighty; and he that ruleth his spirit than he that taketh a city"; "There's beggary in the love that can be reckoned"; "There's the respect that makes calamity of so long life".

We must note, however, that very slight reasons may persuade a writer to prefer *who* or *which* even as the defining relative rather than *that*. Thus, in these last lines of Newbolt's *Clifton Chapel*:

> God send you fortune: yet be sure,
>   Among the lights that gleam and pass,
> You'll live to follow none more pure
>   Than that which glows on yonder brass:
> "*Qui procul hinc*", the legend's writ,—
>   The frontier-grave is far away—
> "*Qui ante diem periit:*
>   *Sed miles, sed pro patria*".

in "lights that gleam" the rule is followed. But in the fourth line the rule would require "Than that that"; and the triple *th* accompanied by the double *that* caused *which* to appear. So in Cleopatra's: "If she first meet the curled Antony he'll make demand of her, and spend that kiss which is my heaven to have", the *which* seems dictated by the preceding *that*. And the reluctance to have a triple *that* brought *which* into the second half of the antithesis: "The good that I would I do not; but the evil which I would not, that I do".

That as defining relative is, after a preposition, replaced by *which*: we have *that* in the third line of Browning's verses below and *o'er which* in the fourth:

> Not on the vulgar mass
> Called "work" must sentence pass,
> Things done that took the eye and had the price,
> O'er which from level stand,
> The low world laid its hand,
> Found straightway to its mind, could value in a trice.

Who and *which*, as relative pronouns, introduce a new

fact rather than a definition. Thus, "My father, who
is in London, will see to it on his return", is the correct
form—not *that*, with commas to mark off the clause introduced by the relative *who*, you notice. So, too, Shelley's
sonnet opens, "I met a traveller from an antique land,
who said, 'Two vast and trunkless legs of stone stand in
the desert' ". We might expand *who* into *and he: who said*
gives a fact about the *traveller*. *Which* in this sentence of
Burke's fulfils the same function: "Surely, never lighted
on this orb, which she hardly seemed to touch, a more
delightful vision."

After all this, it may be well to note that the distinction between *that* as the defining relative and the others
is rather for the class-room and the text-book than for
the actual practice of language. In the main the distinction is ignored.

You notice that the relative may have a different
"case" from that of the noun to which it relates. Here is
Antony's exclamation:

> What, girl! though gray
> Do something mingle with our younger brown,
> yet have we
> A brain that nourishes our nerves and can
> Get goal for goal of youth.

The noun *brain* is in the objective case governed by the
transitive verb *have*. The relative *that*, however, takes its
case from its own clause; and, since it is the subject of the
clause, "that nourishes our nerves", it is in the nominative case. No difficulty arises because of varying case
with *that* or *which*; for the one word serves as nominative
and as objective. Difficulty does arise at times in determining whether the nominative *who* or the objective
whom is needed. Look at Burke's sentence: "I am bold
to say that I ask no ill thing for you, when on parting
from this place I pray that whomever you choose to
succeed me, he may resemble me in all things, except in
my abilities to serve and my fortune to please you."
Whomever is the correct relative; but many of us would
slip into *whoever*.

The following, you will note, need modification: *We feed*

children whom we think are hungry (Write *who*: the
expansion is "We think *they* are hungry"; it is not "We
think them to be hungry"); *I took Cornishmen for choice,
who I knew to be the best sailors in the world* (Write *whom*:
the expansion is "I knew *them* to be").

Report. *What Constitutes a Good Report?*

The answer depends upon the intended purpose of the
report. The report is a clear and complete statement of
what an investigator has found; but, varying with its
purpose, it varies from a bald, uncoloured recital of facts
to a description full of literary graces. Thus, Thackeray's
report of Waterloo would not satisfy a military historian
nor would it be of great service to a military student. It
is an admirable piece of English prose for all that.

> All day long, whilst the women were praying ten
> miles away, the lines of the dauntless English infantry
> were receiving and repelling the furious charges of the
> French horsemen. Guns which were heard at Brussels
> were ploughing up their ranks, and comrades falling,
> and the resolute survivors closing in. Towards evening,
> the attack of the French, repeated and resisted so
> bravely, slackened in its fury. They had other foes
> beside the British to engage, or were preparing for a
> final onset. It came at last: the columns of the Imperial
> Guard marched up the hill of Saint Jean, at length and
> at once to sweep the English from the height which
> they had maintained all day, and spite of all: unscared
> by the thunder of the artillery, which hurled death from
> the English line—the dark rolling column pressed on
> and up the hill. It seemed almost to crest the eminence,
> when it began to waver and falter. Then it stopped,
> still facing the shot. Then at last the English troops
> rushed from the post from which no enemy had been
> able to dislodge them, and the Guard turned and fled.
> No more firing was heard in Brussels—the pursuit
> rolled miles away. Darkness came down on the field
> and city.

With the utilitarian report—the report that serves as a

reliable guide to action in the future, or as acceptable evidence of what took place in the past—we are all familiar. You become a secretary, shall we suppose? Among your duties will be the writing of a report of a meeting: in the minute-book you will write a concise— but yet clear and complete—record of what happened, in particular what decisions were taken. An *aide-memoire* people call the account when they deal with high policy. That is, the matters transacted and the conclusions reached are put on the record lest there should be a future conflict of testimony concerning them. For in diplomacy, it seems more than in other aspects of life, the maxim applies, *Vox perit litera scripta manet*. The spoken word may be distorted, only half-remembered, even wholly forgotten; but the written account endures as a lasting memorial.

As reporter—as minute-taker—your aim is to state, without bias or prejudice, what happened. You will remember Othello's plea:

> I pray you, in your letters,
> When you shall these unlucky deeds relate,
> Speak of me as I am; nothing extenuate,
> Nor set down aught in malice.

You will not colour your account by your own feelings. For when the minutes are confirmed by the appending of the chairman's signature, the preliminary question is, "Do you agree that the minutes as presented are a correct record?"

One ever-present difficulty for the reporter is suggested by a stock phrase of the harassed "official spokesman". How is he to avoid reproach for telling too little or censure for telling too much? His phrase is that things "have gone according to plan". To be precise and definite would be giving information to the enemy; far better use the vague phrase that leaves actual happenings to the imagination.

Reported Speech (Oratio Obliqua). *What are the rules about punctuating Reported Speech?*

The actual words used by a speaker, usually first

person and in the present tense, are marked off by quotation marks ("inverted commas"). When, however, you report the speech—when you turn *oratio recta* into *oratio obliqua*—you leave out the quotation marks. Two examples will make clear the distinction between the two. Here is a little of Stevenson's report in the past tense of an incident in the life of Frances Villon:

> The snow fell over Paris. . . . To poor people, looking up under moist eyebrows, it seemed a wonder where it all came from. Master Francis Villon had propounded an alternative that afternoon, at a tavern window: was it only Pagan Jupiter plucking geese upon Olympus? or were the holy angels moulting? He was only a poor Master of Arts, he went on; and, as the question somewhat touched upon divinity, he durst not venture to conclude.

The direct speech, the actual words, of Master Francis Villon would have been the French equivalent of the reported speech. The punctuation would be:

> Master Francis Villon had propounded an alternative that afternoon, at a tavern window, "Is it," he asked, "only Pagan Jupiter plucking geese upon Olympus? or are the holy angels moulting? I am only," he went on, "a poor Master of Arts; and, as the question somewhat touches upon divinity, I dare not venture to conclude."

And here is a little concerning Mr. Pickwick:

> Mr. Pickwick observed (says the secretary) that fame was dear to the heart of every man. Poetic fame was dear to the heart of his friend Snodgrass; the fame of conquest was equally dear to his friend Tupman; and the desire of earning fame in the sports of the field, the air, and the water, was uppermost in the breast of his friend Wimble.

Re-cast Mr. Pickwick's speech into the first person and the present tense, and you have:

> Mr. Pickwick observed, "Fame is dear to the heart of every man. Poetic fame is dear to the heart of my friend Snodgrass; the fame of conquest is equally dear

to my friend Tupman; and the desire of earning fame in the sports of the field, the air, and the water, is uppermost in the breast of my friend Wimble."

Revision (Its Desirability). *Is there any Benefit from Revision?*

The counsel is at times given that the first version is likely to be the best; revision after revision turns the first sprightly runnings into what is artificial and dull. "Let it go", exclaimed Cobbet; second thoughts are ever the more timid.

Something there may be in this counsel; but prudence and an examination of the good results of revision impel you to reconsider what you have written. This is what Ben Jonson said: "The best writers, in their beginnings, imposed upon themselves care and industry; they did nothing rashly; they obtained first to write correctly, and then custom made it easy and a habit." Here is Pope's method: "Pope was not content to satisfy; he desired to excel; and therefore always endeavoured to do his best: he did not court the candour, but dared the judgment of his reader, and, expecting no indulgence from others, he showed none to himself. He examined lines and words with minute and punctilious observation, and retouched every part with indefatigable diligence, till he left nothing to be forgiven." And here is Dryden's description, probably libellous, of a rival who refused or was unable to revise:

Doeg, without knowing how or why
Made still a blundering kind of melody,
Spurred boldly on, and dashed though thick and thin,
Through sense and nonsense, never out nor in,
He was too warm on picking-work to dwell,
But fagotted his notions as they fell,
And if they rhymed and rattled, all was well.

Look at some instances of successful revision. In the *Ancient Mariner* Coleridge had at first, "The breezes blew, the white foam flew"; he altered it to "The fair breeze flew, the white foam flew". Isn't that better? In the lines so well known from Wordsworth's *Solitary Reaper*,

> No Nightingale did ever chant
> More welcome notes to weary bands
> Of travellers in some shady haunts
> Among Arabian sands

the second line is in place of "So sweetly to reposing bands" and the preposition "among" in the fourth line is in place of "amid". Read the lines aloud in both versions, and you will agree that the version as we know it is the better. One more instance, this from Milton. In *Comus* are the lines:

> A thousand fantasies
> Begin to throng into my memory,
> Of calling shapes, and beckoning shadows dire,
> And airy tongues that syllable men's names.

That last line was at first "And airy tongues that lure night wanderers". Clearly, "lure night wanderers" was rightly rejected for "syllable men's names". Second thoughts are sometimes better.

Rhetoric. *What is Rhetoric?*

Rhetoric is the art of using speech so as to persuade or influence others: Antony's speech—"Friends, Romans, Countrymen"—is a wonderful piece of rhetoric . To men of old rhetoric was an important part of their deliberate study; and it is quite certain that in our own days. though there is much less ostentation about the matter, many give a deal of thought and time to this art of persuading by speech.

Rhetoric is a little suspect among us. We are inclined to class it among the talk hat is designed to mislead us, talk that turns us away from the exercise of calm reason. Moved though we are at the moment, a revulsion may come: we tell ourselves that "His tongue dropped manna, and could make the worse appear the better reason, to perplex and dash maturest counsels". Perhaps that is why the really effective orator poses as none other than a quite ordinary speaker. He disclaims all artifice. He is another Antony cunningly disguising his art. "I am no

orator as Brutus is," he declares, "I am a plain blunt
man that love my friend"; and he continues

> For I have neither wit, nor words, nor worth,
> Action, nor utterance, nor the power of speech,
> To stir men's blood: I only speak right on.

But what a consummate speech Antony made· If you
really want to know what rhetoric is, read the speech again
and again. Simple words he used, but how artfully! See
how he works upon the phrase "For Brutus is an honourable man", his tone varying from what appeared to be
unaffected admiration to savage irony. One other delightful example of such a speech as you would be glad and
proud to make is that of Meninius in the first Act of
Coriolanus.

Indeed, the study of rhetoric is worth while. Wouldn't
you rejoice if it could be said of you what Ben Jonson
said of the great Lord Bacon?—"No man ever spake more
neatly, more pressly, more weightily, or suffered less
emptiness, less idleness, in what he uttered. . . . His
hearers could not cough, or look aside from him, without
loss. He commanded when he spoke; and had his hearers
angry and pleased at his will. No man had their affections
more in his power. The fear of every man that heard him
was, lest he should make an end."

Rhyme. *What Constitutes a Good Rhyme?*

Rhyme is an agreement in the end sounds of words:
joy rhymes with *destroy*, *shutter* with *butter*. The rhyme
is good when the last stressed vowel and any sounds
following that vowel are the same in each of the rhyming
words, but the sound preceding is different. Thus, *smiled*
and *wild*; but *loved* and *proved* only look like rhymes, the
vowel sounds differing.

When the rhyme is of one syllable, it is sometimes
called a "male" or "masculine" rhyme. In these lines of
Pope you have four such rhymes:

> One speaks the Glory of the British Queen,
> And one describes a charming Indian Screen:
> A third interprets Motions, Looks, and Eyes;
> At every Word a Reputation dies.

When the rhyme is of more than one syllable, it is sometimes called a "female" or "feminine" rhyme. In these lines of Browning you have such rhymes:

> This is a spray the Bird clung to,
>   Making it blossom with pleasure,
> Ere the high tree-top she sprung to,
>   Fit for her nest and her treasure.
>   Oh, what a hope beyond measure
> Was the poor spray's, which the flying feet hung to,
> So to be singled out, built in, and sung to!

On occasion a poet will add what are called "internal rhymes" to his end rhymes. Look at these lines of Robert Bridges':

> Wanton with long delay the gay spring leaping cometh;
> The blackthorn starreth now his bough on the eve
>   of May;

> All day in the sweet box-tree the bee for pleasure
>   hummeth:
> The cuckoo sends afloat his note on the air all day.

Notice *delay*, *gay*; *now*, *bough*; *tree*, *bee*; *afloat*, *note*,—all true (good) rhymes.

We all delight in rhyme. Milton did, indeed, claim as a merit for his *Paradise Lost* its freedom from rhyme. "The jingling sound of like endings", he calls it; and he adds, "a fault avoided by the learned ancients both in poetry and all good oratory". But he himself must have delighted in rhyme, and in his shorter poems he has given us charming rhymes in abundance, this in his *Il Penseroso*, for instance:

> Sweet bird, that shunn'st the noise of folly,
> Most musical, most melancholy,
> Thee, chanstress, oft the woods among
> I woo to hear thy even-song.

Rhythm of Prose (Cadence). *Is there a Rhythm of Prose as there is of Poetry?*

Certainly: you do not in your talk continue on the one

stress. At all events, if you do, you are disagreeably monotonous. There is a natural rise and fall—a rhythm or cadence—of the stress. All sentences have some sort of rhythm, though we are apt to apply "rhythmical" only to such sentences as fall into pleasing groups of sounds. Suppose we try to arrange in groups the sounds of a sentence worth calling rhythmical. This of Temple's will serve well: "When all is done, human life is, at the greatest and the best, but like a froward child, that must be played with and humoured a little, to keep it quiet till it falls asleep, and then the care is over." You may not quite agree with the grouping below; but your grouping cannot be greatly different, and you will surely agree that the rhythm is agreeable. Here it is: When all is done/human life/is/at the greatest and the best/but like a froward child/that must be played with/and humoured a little/to keep it quiet/till it falls asleep/and then the care is over/.

Perhaps you have not given much thought to the irregular rhythm of prose. Yet you must often have been displeased in your own composition because of the jerking along like a wagon with ungreased wheels over rough ground, or because of a flight of short unaccented syllables, or because of a huddle of heavy syllables. "It reads badly," you say; and, wisely, you set about remodelling it. Well, the remodelling will come more easily and be more effective through your close study of sentences like the one examined. Other instances in plenty you will find in the quotations up and down this book.

Right Word (The). *What Considerations should Guide in Choosing Words?*

The English language does in fact often present us with many words more or less applicable to our purpose. Which of these is the right word? The answer seems to suggest itself when you think of the work of language—of speech and of writing. That work is to carry thought from mind to mind. The words in which you embody

your thought should serve to carry that thought un-
impaired into the minds of those to whom you speak or for
whom you write.

First of all, then, the word should be one the meaning
of which you yourself know well. Secondly, it should be
one that your audience will be able, readily and certainly,
to interpret in the very sense intended by you. Therefore
it is that you select an easy word rather than a difficult
one, a short word rather than a long one.

You will know, though, that the choice is governed by
taste: what seems the better word to you may not seem
so to another, quite as well qualified to judge. This must
be so. The choice among possible substitutes is nearly
always a choice between better and worse, not between
right and wrong. It may be, in making language do the
journey-work of men, we do foolishly in troubling greatly
about the choice. Better get on with the job. Perhaps
you remember Barrie's *Sentimental Tommy*. All expected
him to win the essay competition; but he wrote hardly a
score of words:

> He had brought himself to public scorn for lack of a
> word. What word? they asked testily, but even now
> he could not tell. He had wanted a Scotch word that
> would signify how many people were in church, and it
> was on the tip of his tongue but would come no further.
> Puckle was nearly the word, but it did not mean as
> many people as he meant. The hour had gone by just
> like winking; he had forgotten all about time while
> searching his mind for the word.

Consideration for those who are to interpret our words
suggests that we should avoid slang, the base coin of
language; that we should be sparing indeed in using
foreign phrases, out-of-the-way terms of science, allusions
to things unfamiliar; and that we should curb our appetite for elaboration. For we cannot be certain that these
will be speedily interpreted in the meaning we intend.
One example may be welcome. It is from an official report
on a tribe of Indians called Gonds. The thought to be
put into words was "Gonds drink, but seldom get drunk",

D

—six words, five of which are words of the street and market place. Is the elaborate verbiage of the report an improvement?—"The members of this aboriginal tribe are notoriously addicted to the consumption of alcoholic stimulants but rarely, if ever, prolong their potations to the point at which intoxication supervenes." [See more under Synonyms.]

Semi-colon and Comma. *How are we to Determine whether the pause needs a Comma or a Semi-colon?*

The comma indicates a short pause in a sentence, the group of words marked off by a comma being usually a small one. The semi-colon indicates a longer, a more impressive pause. A study of instances will make the distinction clear. Look at this little paragraph of Macaulay's:

> Meantime the tide was rising fast. The Mountjoy began to move, and soon passed safe through the broken stakes and floating spars. But her brave master was no more. A shot from one of the batteries had struck him; and he died by the most enviable of all deaths, in sight of the city which was his birthplace, which was his home, and which had just been saved by his courage and self-devotion from the most frightful form of destruction.

Two short sentences, the first and the third, need no internal stops. In the second sentence, "The Mountjoy ... spars", the comma marks a pause between the two co-ordinate clauses, though many modern writers would dispense with that comma. Still, it is advisable to have it in order to make a distinction between the *and* joining sentences and the *and* joining phrases. In the fourth sentence Macaulay wishes you to make a more impressive pause after *him* than after *and* in the second sentence. He, therefore, uses a semi-colon, contenting himself with commas in the enumeration that follows.

The semi-colon is better than the comma, you note, when you have together two sentences presenting a contrast. Thus:

Give a man the secure possession of a bleak **rock,** and he will turn it into a garden; give him a nine years' lease of a garden, and he will convert it into a desert.

Some would make two separate sentences, separated by a full-stop, of this. But the antithesis is more effective so presented.

It may perhaps be noted that the semi-colon seems to be going the way of the colon, and that writers will shortly restrict themselves to commas and full-stops, with an occasional question-mark when called for. This seems to be a pity.

Sentences (Kinds). *Is it possible to place sentences into definite classes?*

We can do this with some measure of accuracy. We define a written sentence as the portion of writing from one full-stop to another; and this usually corresponds to the expression in speech of one thought. The sentence puts into fit words a statement, a question, a command, or a prayer; and it usually has a subject, about which it is built, and a predicate, expressing the thought about that subject.

The *simple sentence* has one subject and one predicate. Here are examples:

(*a*) A word fitly spoken /is like apples of gold in pictures
      (Subject)   of silver
                               (Predicate)

(*b*) Sorrow and sighing /shall flee.

(*c*) She sat like patience on a monument smiling at grief.

(*d*) Fear no more the heat of the sun.

(*e*) Astonished grief had swept over the country.

The *complex sentence* contains one or more dependent clauses. Here are examples:

(*a*) When, two days previously, the news of the approaching end had been made public, astonished grief had swept the country. [Here the clause "When . . .

public" is an expansion of an adverb like *then*, and is called an Adverbial Clause.]

(*b*) The vast majority of her subjects had never known a time when Queen Victoria had not been reigning over them. [Here the clause "when . . . them" specifies or defines *time*, and is an expansion of *such* and it is therefore called an Adjectival Clause.]

(*c*) That they were about to lose her appeared a scarcely possible thought. [Here the clause "that they . . . lose her" is equivalent to "this fact": it is a Noun Clause.]

The *compound sentence* consists of two or more sentences which could have stood separately, but are put together as a combined thought. This is one: "So, taking care not to tread on the grass, we will go along the straight walk to the west front, and there stand for a while, looking up at its deep-pointed porches."

A less accurate but more useful classing of sentences is into *loose* and *compact*. To call a sentence loose does not, it must be emphasized, imply condemnation. Some loose sentences are very delightful and very fitting. It is as though the speaker, or the writer, asks us to watch the developing of his thought. For it develops as he expresses it; he adds a new fact, softens a previous assertion, modifies a too confident prediction. *And, but, though, if,* —these and like joining words carry the thought along, the thought that might choose several ending-places. Probably in our formal business writing, where precise and concise expression is so desirable, we shall avoid sentences loosely built. But how fit such sentences are for leisurely reading, for entertaining gossip, for gentle moralizing. Here is one: "A crowd is not company, and faces are but a gallery of pictures, and talk but a tinkling cymbal where there is no love." See how Charles Lamb takes you into his confidence; look at a little of his playful comment upon himself:

Few understood him, and I am not certain that at all times he quite understood himself. He too much affected that dangerous figure—irony. He sowed doubtful speeches and reaped plain, unequivocal hatred. He would interrupt the gravest discussion with some light jest, and yet, perhaps, not quite irrelevant in ears that could understand it. Your long and much talkers hated him. The informal habit of his mind joined to an inveterate impediment of speech, forbade him to be an orator, and he seemed determined that no one else should play that part when he was present. He was *petit* and ordinary in his person and appearance. I have seen him in what is called good company, but when he has been a stranger, sit silent, and be suspected for an odd fellow, till, some unlucky occasion provoking it, he would stutter out some senseless pun (not altogether senseless, perhaps, if rightly taken), which has stamped his character for the evening.

Some sentences are closely built: till you reach the end, the full-stop, the thought is not complete. It is as though thought and expression spring complete together. Such a well-girt sentence is this from a *Times* leader: "The reasonable requirement that parents of evacuated children should contribute to their maintenance comes to-day into force." You agree that the sentence would be looser if the expansion of "requirement" were added as a kind of afterthought: "The reasonable requirement comes to-day into force that parents of evacuated children should contribute to their maintenance."

Try your hand at tightening up a few loose sentences. This is one from the same leader: "There is no valid reason why the requirement should adversely affect the dispersal of the children,—provided, of course, that the administration is tactful and a fair view is taken of those on whom the charge is placed." The proviso introduced by the dash shakes your mind from the state of rest you had reached. Your mind had been carried smoothly from *There* to *children*. You were prepared to acquiesce or to deny; and the proviso, suddenly shot at you, makes you reconsider. Try the effect of beginning with the proviso and omitting the patronizing "of course": "Provided that . . .placed, there is . . . children."

Here is another: "The evacuation scheme was not designed to relieve parents of natural responsibilities, nor should it be allowed to do so when the ability to pay is unquestionable." Try the effect of bringing the limiting clause, "when the ability to pay is unquestionable," into the structure of the sentence. Thus: "The evacuation scheme was not designed to relieve parents of natural responsibilities; nor, when the ability to pay is unquestionable, should it be allowed to do so."

Should this sentence be more closely girt?—"The king fell from his horse and died two hours after the fall, which was occasioned by the horse's stumbling on a mole-hill, while he was on his return from reviewing his troops."

Sentences (Length):   *How long should a sentence be?*

Question may arise regarding the desirable length of sentences. The modern tendency is towards short, crisp sentences; but there is no reluctance to have a long sentence, where that appears called for. Indeed, the nature of the writing will dictate the kind of sentence. Consider, for example, Froude's account of the pursuit of the treasure-ship. Long-drawn-out sentences would have been unsuitable. Reading the rapid utterances, we seem to be panting to keep up with the thrilling chase.

Drake began to realize that he was now entirely alone, and had only himself and his own crew to depend on. There was nothing to do but to go through with it, danger adding to the interest. Arica was the next point visited. Half a hundred blocks of silver were picked up at Arica. After Arica came Lima, the chief depot of all, where the greatest haul was looked for. At Lima, alas! they were just too late. Twelve great hulks were anchored there. The sails were unbent, the men were ashore. They contained nothing but some chests of reals and a few bales of silks and linen. But a thirteenth called the *Cacafuego*, had sailed a few days before for the isthmus, with the whole produce of the Lima mines for the season. Her ballast was silver, her cargo gold and emeralds and rubies.

Drake deliberately cut the cables of the ships in the Roads, that they might drive ashore and be unable to follow him. The *Pelican* spread her wings, every feather of them, and sped away in pursuit. He would know the *Cacafuego*, so he learnt at Lima, by the peculiar cut of her sails. The first man who caught sight of her was promised a gold chain for his reward. A sail was seen on the second day. It was not the chase, but it was worth stopping for. Eighty pounds' weight of gold was found, and a great gold crucifix, set with emeralds said to be as large as pigeon's eggs. They took the kernel. They left the shell. Still on and on. We learn from the Spanish accounts that the Viceroy of Lima, as soon as he recovered from his astonishment, dispatched ships in pursuit. They came up with the last plundered vessel, heard terrible tales of the rovers' strength, and went back for a larger force. The *Pelican* meanwhile went along upon her course for 800 miles. At length, when in the latitude of Quito and close under the shore, the *Cacafuego's* peculiar sails were sighted, and the gold chain was claimed. There she was, freighted with the fruit of Aladdin's garden, going lazily along a few miles ahead. Care was needed in approaching her. If she guessed the *Pelican's* character, she would run in upon the land and they would lose her. It was afternoon. The sun was still above the horizon, and Drake meant to wait till night, when the breeze would be off the shore, as in the tropics it always is.

The *Pelican* sailed two feet to the *Cacafuego's* one Drake filled his empty wine-skins with water and trailed them astern to stop his way. The chase supposed that she was followed by some heavy-loaded trader, and, wishing for company on a lonely voyage, she slackened sail and waited for him to come up. At length the sun went down into the ocean, the rosy light faded from off the snows of the Andes; and, when both ships had become invisible from the shore, the skins were hauled in, the night wind rose, and the water began to ripple under the *Pelican's* bows. The *Cacafuego* was swiftly overtaken, and when within a cable's length a voice hailed her to put her head into the wind. The Spanish commander, not understanding so strange an order, held on his course. A broadside brought down his mainyard, and a flight of arrows rattled on his deck. He was himself wounded. In a few minutes he was a prisoner, and the ship and her precious freight were in the corsair's power. The wreck was cut away; the ship was cleared; a prize crew was put on board. Both vessels turned their heads to the sea. At daybreak no land was to be seen, and the examination of the prize began. The full value was never acknowledged. The invoice, if there was one, was destroyed. The accurate figures were known only to Drake and Queen Elizabeth. A published schedule acknowledged to twenty tons of silver bullion, thirteen chests of silver coins, and a hundredweight of gold, but there were gold nuggets besides in indefinite quantity, and "a great store" of pearls, emeralds, and diamonds. The Spanish Government proved a loss of a million and a half ducats, excluding what belonged to private persons. The total capture was immeasurably greater.

Contrast with these swift sentences the stately periods in which Gibbon describes the Roman roads, directed straight from the imperial city to the bounds of empire:

All these cities were connected with each other, and with the capital, by the public highways, which, issuing from the Forum of Rome, traversed Italy, pervaded the provinces, and were terminated only by the frontiers of the empire. If we carefully trace the distance from the wall of Antoninus to Rome, and from thence to Jerusalem, it will be found that the great chain of communication, from the north-west to the south-east point of the empire, was drawn out to the length of four thousand and eighty Roman miles. The public roads were accurately divided by milestones, and ran in a direct line from one city to another, with very little respect for the obstacles either of nature or private property. Mountains were perforated, and bold arches thrown over the broadest and most rapid streams. The middle part of the road was raised into a terrace which commanded the adjacent country, consisted of several strata of sand, gravel, and cement, and was paved with large stones, or, in some places near the capital, with

granite. Such was the solid construction of the Roman
highways, whose firmness has not entirely yielded to the
effort of fifteen generations. They united the subjects
of the most distant provinces by an easy and familiar
intercourse; but their primary object had been to
facilitate the marches of the legions; nor was any
country considered as completely subdued, till it had
been rendered, in all its parts, pervious to the arms and
authority of the conqueror. The advantage of receiving
the earliest intelligence, and of conveying their orders
with celerity, induced the emperors to establish
throughout their extensive dominions the regular
institution of posts. Houses were everywhere erected
at the distance only of five or six miles; each of them
was constantly provided with forty horses, and by the
help of these relays it was easy to travel a hundred miles
in a day along the Roman roads. The use of posts was
allowed to those who claimed it by an imperial mandate;
but although originally intended for the public service, it
was sometimes indulged to the business or conveniency
of private citizens. Nor was the communication of the
Roman empire less free and open by sea than it was
by land. The provinces surrounded and enclosed the
Mediterranean: and Italy, in the shape of an immense
promontory, advanced into the midst of that great
lake. The coasts of Italy are, in general, destitute of
safe harbours; but human industry had corrected the
deficiencies of nature; and the artificial port of Ostia,
in particular, situate at the mouth of the Tiber, and
formed by the Emperor Claudius, was a useful monument of Roman greatness. From the port, which was
only sixteen miles from the capital, a favourable breeze
frequently carried vessels in seven days to the Columns
of Hercules, and in nine or ten to Alexandria in Egypt.
—*Decline and Fall of the Roman Empire.*

"Shall" or "Will"? *Are there rules to determine when "Shall" is the better word, when "Will"?*

Here is another of the points where the teachings in the
class-room are, for the most part, ignored outside the
class-room,—ignored maybe by the teacher himself.

As with other points this is a pity. Still, so far as language is concerned, what people think to be right is right. Horace long ago said that Usage determines matters of language; in the hands of Usage is the right and rule of speech. He was, indeed, speaking of words that flourish and fade; but what he said applies also to the manner of using those words:

Multa renascentur quae jam cecidire, cadentque
Quae nunc in honore vocabula, si volet usus,
Quem penes arbitrium est et jus et norma loquendi.

[Many a word that has become old-fashioned, even obsolete, will have a new birth; and many a word now in high honour will as time passes be neglected. It all depends on Custom; for in the hands of Custom is the arbitrament, the right and rule of speech.]

These, then, are class-room rules; but, we should hasten to add, adherence to the rules adds to the grace and to the accuracy of language. Start with that story of Barrie's. The clever young Scotsman had been offered what many eagerly sought, regular work as leader writer for a great newspaper. He was elated. But he hid his elation; and the Editor proceeded: "By the way, you are Scotch, I think." "Yes," said Rob. "I only asked," the editor explained, "because of the *shall* and *will* difficulty. Have you got over that yet?" "No," said Rob, sadly, "and never will." "I shall warn the proof-readers to be on the alert," Mr. Rowbottom said, laughing, though Rob did not see why.

The Southerner very likely has no trouble about the matter. "I never shall" comes trippingly to the tongue when the statement is of futurity, uncoloured by an implication of resolve. Look at the distinction between the sense of "we shall" (simple futurity) in the Addison sentence and the sense of "I will" (futurity plus resolve) in the Thackeray sentence:

When I read the several dates of the tombs, of some that died yesterday and some six hundred years ago, I consider that great day when we shall all of us be contemporaries and make our appearance together.

(*Essays.*)

"I will see her," said Arthur. "I'll ask her to marry me once more. I *will*. No one shall prevent me."

Look, too, at this illustration from one of Mr. Churchill's war speeches: "We shall not fail or falter; we shall not weaken or tire. Neither the sudden shock of battle nor the long drawn trials of vigilance and exertion will wear us down." *Shall*, you agree,—the matter of fact statement of what the future will bring, a statement needing no emphasis and put forward as admitting of no doubt— is better for the first personal pronoun than *will*. You agree, too, that *will* is better than *shall* for the verb attendant upon *shock* and *trials*. The calm declaration would be spoiled by *shall*; for *shall* would here suggest bluster.

The rule for the expression of *simple futurity* is, therefore, this: for the first person (*I* and *we*) the auxiliary is *shall*; for the second and third persons (*thou, you; he, she, they*) the auxiliary is *will*. Examples are:

> I shall not see the shadows,
>   I shall not feel the rain;
> I shall not hear the nightingale
>   Sing on, as if in pain.
> [*Shall*, first person, futurity only.]

"We shall see what we are when we come to Castlewood." [*Shall*, first person, futurity only.]

"Where shall we put the key?" [*Shall*, first person, futurity only.]

"Will the day's journey take the whole long day?" [*Will*, third person, futurity only.]

"They will not keep you waiting at that door." [*Will*, third person, futurity only.]

When, however, futurity is accompanied by an implied statement of resolution, or compulsion, or prophecy— we have *will* in the first person, *shall* in the second and third. Examples are:

"I will arise and go now." [*Will*, first person, futurity and also determination.]

"Thou shalt love thy neighbour." [*Shalt*, second person, futurity and also command.]

"The truth is great, and shall prevail." [*Shall*, third person, futurity and also prophecy.]

"We here highly resolve that these dead shall not have died in vain; that this nation, under God, shall have a new birth of freedom; and that government of the people, by the people, and for the people, shall not perish from the earth." [*Shall*, third person, futurity and also resolution.]

> They shall grow not old, as we that are left grow old;
> Age shall not weary them, nor the years condemn,
> At the going down of the sun and in the morning
> We will remember them.
>
> (Laurence Binyon *For the Fallen*)

We must remember that *will* is at times an independent verb, meaning *should like* or *would like*. Contrast, for example, the meanings in these lines of Matthew Arnold:

> His mates had arts to rule as they desired
>   The workings of men's brains;
> And they can bind them to what thoughts they will:
> "And I," he said, "the secret of their art,
>   When fully learned, will to the world impart:
> But it needs Heaven-sent moments for this skill."

In the third line *will* is *wish*, *would like*; in the fifth line *will* is the future coloured by a promise.

Examine, finally, these instances:

(1) Which of these is the statement of simple futurity which implies a threat also?:

  (*a*) I shall see him to-morrow, when he will tell me all about it.

  (*b*) I will see him to-morrow, when he shall tell me all about it.

(2) Which of these is the statement of simple futurity, which is what one determined upon suicide might have said?:

  (*a*) I shall drown, and nobody will save me.

  (*b*) I will drown, and nobody shall save me.

"Should" or "Would"? *Do the rules about "Shall"
and "Will" apply also to "Should" and "Would"?*

In the main they do. To express the conditional mood,
without other modification, we have *should* in the first
person, *would* in the second and third. Examples are:
(1) "If you would sit thus by me every night, I should
work better, do you comprehend?" (2) "I should be in
time if I hurried." (3) "I would injure no man, and
accordingly I should provide no resentment." [*I would*
adds to *I should* the idea of wish or intention.]

A writer to *The Times* puts the distinction cleverly:

> I should like to endorse your correspondent's com-
> plaint of the growing misuse of "will' and "shall". In
> particular I would protest against the common mistake,
> even the announcers of the B.B.C. frequently make of
> saying "I would like to say", when they mean "I
> would say" or "I should like to say". "I would"
> means "I should like". "I would like to say" means,
> therefore, "I should like to like to say" or "I wish I
> liked saying", which is clearly not what they would say
> and therefore not what they *should* say, as they ob-
> viously enjoy having their say. A distinguished critic
> from Ireland, in taking us Englishmen to task for our
> mispronunciation of our own language, asked, "Would
> we understand Shakespeare if we had a record of his
> voice and could produce it in a gramophone?" Of
> course we would, if we could, but the question is
> whether we should.

If you have followed that entertaining exposition, you
should have no further trouble about the matter. Perhaps you will enjoy this little passage from *Northanger
Abbey*, where Jane Austen supplies you with some good
examples of how to use *shall* and *will*, *should* and *would*:

> "Do you know, there are two odious young men who
> have been staring at me this half-hour. They really put
> me quite out of countenance. Let us go and look at the
> arrivals. They will hardly follow us there."
> Away they walked to the book; and, while Isabella
> examined the names, it was Catherine's employment to
> watch the proceedings of these alarming young men.

"They are not coming this way, are they? I hope
they are not so impertinent as to follow us. Pray let
me know if they are coming. I am determined I will
not look up."

In a few moments Catherine, with unaffected pleasure, assured her that she need be no longer uneasy, as
the gentlemen had just left the Pump-room.

"And which way are they gone?" said Isabella,
turning hastily round. "One was a very good-looking
young man."

"They went towards the churchyard."

"Well, I am amazingly glad I have got rid of them.
And now, what say you to going to Edgar Buildings
with me, and looking at my new hat? You said you
should like to see it."

Catherine readily agreed. "Only," she added,
"perhaps we may overtake the two young men."

"Oh! never mind that. If we make haste, we shall
pass by them presently, and I am dying to show you
my hat."

"But if we only wait a few minutes, there will be
no danger of our seeing them at all."

"I shall not pay them any such compliment, I assure
you. I have no notion of treating men with such respect
That is the way to spoil them."

[Catherine had said, "I should like"; Isabella reports it
retaining the *should*. Compare the sentence: "Let no one
feel confident that he should have escaped the delusion
if he had lived at the time when it prevailed."]

Silent Letters. *Why do we retain, in spelling English words, Letters Unsounded?*

We can advance no very convincing reason. Some note
of how these silent letters have come about may explain
though not justify their presence. That they present
difficulties is certain. The schoolmistress bought salmon,
and the assistant wrote on her bill "sammon". She
disliked this spelling, and remonstrated. "Sorry, madam,"
said the cashier, "I've spoken before about his spelling.

They don't teach 'em to-day in school like they used to when you and me was young." And he altered the word to "psalmon".

On the whole the letters of English words give reliable guidance to the sounds; but the doubt that sometimes arises causes much trouble. Very likely you know that curious collection—"Though the tough cough and hiccough plough me through"—devised to show the varied sounds for which *ough* stands. There you have six sounds—*o, uff, off, up, ow, oo*—for the one symbol, And words like *biscuits* (kits), *circuit* (serket), *salmon* (samn), *debt* (det), *delight* (de-lite), *psalm* (sahm), *deign* (dan), *rhyme* (rim), *fissure* (fisher), *leopard* (lep-ard), *yeoman* (yo-man), cause confusion.

At times the now silent letter serves to connect an English word with its equivalent in another language. *Salmon* itself is an instance. Like many of our words denoting dishes for the table—words like *beef, mutton, veal, pork*—the word came with the Normans; and, like the modern French *saumon*, it was long without the *l*. But when people began to study the origins of words and found that in Latin the *l* appeared—appeared because it stood for a sound—they inserted the *l* in the English word, too. The silent letters in the words *debt* and *receipt* are similar. *Debt* had no *b* in Chaucer's time. The learned, about the time when printing began to crystallize spelling, introduced the *b* lest the connective of *debt* and *debtor* with the Latin *debitum* should be overlooked. (Compare the words *debit* and *debenture*, where the *b* is both seen and heard.) So it was with *receipt*. In the first edition of Bacon's *Essays* we have "Every defect of the mind may have a special receit". The *p* was inserted to bring *receipt* into line with words like *receptacle* and *recipient*.

The silent *p* in words like *psalm* and *psalter*, which came into English at a very early date, also results from learned revision. It was to show Grecian origin. In other words, more recently taken from the Greek, the *p* has always been there, though very likely never sounded. Such are words like *psychology*, the study of the workings of men's minds, and *pseudonym*, the pen-name assumed by a writer.

The silent *t* is curious. Compare the noun *nestling* (where *t* is usually sounded) with the verb *nestle* (where *t* is silent). When *nestle* was a word of two syllables, the *t* of *nest* could easily be pronounced; when *nestle* became a word of one syllable (*nesl*) the *t* sound vanished. And now we have a number of words similarly written with the silent *t*: *bristle, castle, hostler, Christmas, wrestle, apostle, bustle* (which rhymes with *muscle*), and *waltz* (which should rhyme with *false*), though the sight of the *t* at times evokes the sound. So in words like *fasten*: two syllables are telescoped into one and in the process the *t* sound vanishes: *hasten, glisten, listen, christen, chestnut,* and so on.

The silent letter occurring most often,—the silent *e* in words like *whole, were, have, there, purpose, mere, alone*— has varied origins. Usually it remains as a silent reminder of a lost inflexion. It has varied duties, too. In some words it tells us that the preceding vowel is a long one. Contrast *rat* with *rate, bar* with *bare, sit* with *site, not* with *note, cut* with *cute.*

Similes. *What Guides are there to the use of Illustrations in Speech or in Writing?*

Well, when a teacher would have you grasp a new idea, he tries to link it with an old idea. He compares; he brings into mind a likeness, a simile. Thus, Virgil wants you to have a clear picture of the shades on the bank of the inevitable river; and this is his method:

As in the forests the leaves fall from the trees at the first frosts of Autumn, or as the birds flock shorewards from the deep when the cold of the year sends them fleeing over the sea to sunny lands, so the shades stood, each praying for the first·passage over, and they stretched out their hands in longing for the farther shore.

The illustration is a lighting-up, an illumination: it makes clear by way of example. The seen, tangible thing may, for instance, impress the thought of the unseen intangible thing. Thus:

Blessed is the man that findeth wisdom and getteth understanding; for the merchandise thereof is better than silver, and the gain thereof better than gold; it is more precious than pearls, and all things thou canst desire are not to be compared to her.

Or this, where an old writer makes ingenious apology for his mingling of sound teaching with pleasant entertainment:

These my writings, I hope, shall taste like gilded pills, which are so composed as well to tempt the appetite and deceive the palate as to help and medicinally work upon the whole body; my lines shall not only recreate but rectify the mind.

Or again: the theme, that the glories of our blood and state are shadows not substantial things, is ages old; it gains new freshness by the comparison:

The Worldly Hope men set their Hearts upon
  Turns Ashes—or it prospers; and anon,
Like Snow upon the Desert's dusty Face,
  Lighting a little Hour or two—is gone.

To make understanding easy is one reason—an important reason, too—for the comparisons, the similes, we meet with in our reading. Another reason there is; and this is also important. The well-chosen comparison adds to enjoyment, whether it is added as a tasteful ornament or just for the fun of the thing. For we need not give unqualified assent to Doctor Johnson's dictum: "A simile, to be perfect, must both illustrate and ennoble the subject." You cannot hold that the simile in this couplet ennobles its subject.

And like a lobster boiled, the morn
From black to red began to turn.

The strange comparison is very different from that implied in

But, look, the morn, in russet mantle clad,
Walks o'er the dew on yon high eastern hill.

Yet, in some moods, you rejoice in the unexpected simile.

The illustration, added as ornament, may indeed bring a less familiar—not a more familiar—idea into mind. There is that fanciful simile in the opening lines of Shelley's *Ode to the West Wind*:

> Those from whose unseen presence the leaves dead
> Are driven like ghosts from an enchanter fleeing.

The swirling leaves of October are better known to you than the expelled spirits. And the likelihood is that you have seen the twisted trunks of trees more often than intertwined snakes. But you welcome the simile:

> We paused among the pines that stood!
> The giants of the waste,
> Tortured by storms to shapes as rude
> As serpents interlaced.

Simplicity. *Why are we urged to be Simple in our Language?*

The reason rests in the very nature of language. When we speak or write, we ask for the co-operation of hearer or writer: two minds at least must work if language is to carry thought. It is foolish, however, to ask for great exertion from hearer or reader. It is discourtesy, too. Good manners as well as good sense tell us to make our meaning easy of access. Making it so, we select the simple word when it fully expresses our meaning. In *Alice in Wonderland* you read upon the point:

> "In that case," said the Dodo, solemnly rising to its feet, "I move that the meeting adjourn for the immediate adoption of more energetic remedies."
>
> "Speak English!" said the Eaglet. "I don't know the meaning of half those long words, and what's more, I don't believe you do either!"

Many a time you have echoed in your mind the Eaglet's energetic protest. The speaker is more intent upon exhibiting his command of long words—more concerned about his manner of speaking—than about informing your mind. He has forgotten, if ever he knew it, that language calls for co-operation. English is as good a vehicle of thought as there is; but this is dependent upon the hearer's ability to interpret correctly. A really effective speaker knows this well. "Will the Press be admitted to General Smutt's speech?" was the question put to the Prime Minister. "Yes," he said, not, as many of his predecessors in office would have said, "The answer is in the affirmative".

When we speak without elaborate preparation, when we are moved by sudden impulse, we speak in words that can be understood. The pity is that, so very often, when we write or when we make a formal speech, simplicity goes. The touch of the pen puts constraint upon us; we, quite mistakenly, cast about for more elevated terms than came naturally in our extempore speech. Then we called a spade a spade; we thought rather of what we would say than of the manner in which to say it. So doing we spoke with effect. Through misapplied labour our first sprightly runnings become heavy and laboured.

Indeed, the idea that a simple directness needs elaboration—the idea that it lacks something of the grandeur of literature—leads at times to strange pranks. Thus, the version we all know and admire is:

A certain man had two sons. And the younger of them said to his father, "Father, give me the portion of goods that falleth to me".

Are there really people who prefer the woolly, pretentious version?—

A gentleman of splendid family and opulent fortune had two sons. One day the younger approached his father, and begged him in the most importunate and soothing terms to make a partition of his effects.

Singular or Plural ? *Is the word "Means" Singular or Plural?*

As with other of our words "means" is misleading: it looks like a plural, it is a singular. We say "A means of overcoming the difficulty was found" (*a* and *was*). "As she carried no flag, there was no means of instantly ascertaining whether she had struck" (*was* not *were*). *Summons* is similar: "The summons bids you attend the court" (not *bid*); "A heavy summons lies like lead upon me" (*lies* not *lie*). *News*, though sometimes used as a plural—Shelley wrote "There are bad news from Palermo"—is also, as a rule, looked upon as a singular noun. Here are instances: "For evil news rides fast while good news waits", "Ill news hath wings and with the wind doth go, Comfort's a cripple and comes ever slow", "As cold waters to a thirsty soul so is good news from a far country", "Lady Middleton exerted herself to ask Mr. Palmer if there was any news in the paper. 'No, none at all,' he replied, and read on." The *s* in *alms* is not the plural inflexion; and *alms* is used as a singular in "Seeing Peter and John about to go into the Temple, he asked an alms". There is now a reluctance to use *alms* other than as a plural.

The names of sciences like *ethics, economics, mechanics, politics* are, as a rule, looked on as singular nouns: "Mechanics is essential for the engineer" (*is* not *are*).

Slang (Jargon). *Is any defence available for the use of Slang?*

Perhaps you may put up a weak defence. With your familiars, and for the fun of the thing, you may delight in using a jargon diverging more or less from "King's English". To contrast better the English of cultured people with a lapse into the colloquial, serves the dramatist well: "They say," said Eliza, 'he died of influenza; but I believe they done 'im in." This slang or jargon is a kind of secret language, readily interpreted by you and your fellow-users, but only guessed at by outsiders. Margaret, in *Fanny's First Play*, says things like "Don't funk answering", "This is a let-down for me", "What did you do to the copper?" And her mother, grieving at the colloquial *funk* and *let-down* and *copper*, might ask her not to use such "slang". For, to be sure, it is ill mannered to speak in a tongue not understood by all of the company.

The slang, again, may be an intended mockery of

formal propriety, a conscious offence against recognized usage. The user of the slang would have no trouble in expressing his meaning in terms that all would approve of. But the slang term seems livelier and out it comes. Thus, a first-class ship in Lloyd's Register is "A1"; it is an easy transit to call a dinner of which one heartily approves "A1", too. The speaker is resolved; and he might say, "Well I'll do it". But that is tame; so "Here goes", he says.

It is true, also, that we cannot always tell whether a word or a phrase is to be classed as Standard English, or as slang—the base coin of language. For English is not a fixed language. A fixed language is dead; and our language is very much alive, is constantly adopting new words and adapting old ones to new meanings. These words, for instance, *phiz, chap, cab. mob, bus,* were at the outset slang shortenings of *physionomy, chapman* (meaning "dealer"), *cabriolet, mobile vulgus* ("the fickle multitude"), and *omnibus* ("for all and everybody"). Three of them, *cab* and *mob* and *bus,* have now lived down their slang origin, and are recognized in polite society; the other two, *phiz* and *chap,* are still outsiders. Slang is like rebellion in this: when it is successful, none presumes to call it slang.

When all is said, however, that can be said in defence of slang, it seems deplorable to desert without need the genuine for the spurious. And the user of slang may well lose track with the truth of things. "Where d'jer get it?" asks one London urchin of another. "I knocked it orff" is the answer. "I stole it" would be self-condemnation, but very likely a salutary self-condemnation.

Sound (A CONSIDERATION IN COMPOSITION). *Are we wise to consider the Sounds as well as the Meanings of the Words we use?*

We are very wise to do so. For we are to remember that language is a toy as well as a tool. It gives delight as well as serves a useful purpose; and the speakers and writers who wish to be really effective have regard to both aspects of language. Perhaps, indeed, we have a right to expect pleasure from what we hear or read. Miss Mitford evidently thought so: she wrote of Scott's *Waverley*: "There is not in the whole book one single page of pure and vernacular English, one single period of which you forget the sense in admiration of the sound."

Consider a few short passages in which the writers have, clearly, given thought about sounds as well as about sense. Here are two lines of Wordsworth's: "And from the turf a fountain broke and gurgled at our feet." Reading this aloud you note the repeated letters *g* and *f*. The throat-letter—the guttural *g*—seems apt for words like *gurgle*, *giggle*, *struggle*, *wriggle*. The gushing *f* sound is similarly apt for words like *foam*, *froth*, *front*, *fount*. Wordsworth makes his lines effective by the use of these letters.

Now read aloud these five lines from Tennyson's *Lotus Eaters*:

> All round the coast the languid air did swoon
> Breathing like one that hath a weary dream.
> Full-faced above the valley stood the moon;
> And, like a downward smoke, the slender stream
> Along the cliff to fall and pause and fall did seem.

Tennyson always took great care with the sounds of his words. "I had rather," he said, "lose a thought than get two s's together." In *The Lotus Eaters* he wants his words to suggest care-soothing sleep. Note, among the other devices by which he effects his purpose, how each line of the passage above dies languidly away in an *m* or an *n* sound.

Even a cursory reading makes you aware of the cunning arrangement of sounds in this paragraph:

> Arise, shine; for thy light is come, and the glory of the Lord is risen upon thee. For, behold, the darkness shall cover the earth, and gross darkness the people; but the Lord shall arise upon thee, and his glory shall be seen upon thee, And the Gentiles shall come to thy light, and kings to the brightness of thy rising. . . . The sun shall be no more thy light by day; neither for brightness shall the moon give light unto thee: but the

Lord shall be to thee an everlasting light, and thy God thy glory. Thy sun shall no more go down; neither shall thy moon withdraw herself: for the Lord shall be thine everlasting light, and the days of thy mourning shall be ended.

The meaning of this passage is important enough; but fix your attention for a while upon the sounds and the arrangement of the sounds. Read the passage aloud twice or thrice. That invocation—"Arise, shine; for thy light is come"—is like a clarion call. What makes it so effective? Isn't the main cause the long vowel *i*, repeated four times in the seven words? This sound runs through the passages now faintly among other vowel sounds, now ringing out in jubilation. In the second sentence—"For, behold, the darkness shall cover the earth, and gross darkness the people; but the Lord shall arise upon thee, and his glory shall be seen upon thee"—you hear it once only. But how it rings out in the next sentence—"And the Gentiles shall come to thy light, and kings to the brightness of thy rising".

The undertone—the *or* sound of *glory, Lord, for, more, mourning*—gives the needed foil to the long *i* sound. And look at the dying close where the exhilarating sounds are followed by sounds of peace and rest: "The Lord shall be thine everlasting light, and the days of thy mourning shall be ended." You will yourself note other happy unions of sounds in the passage; and, when you have studied the sounds, very likely you will return to the sense of the passage with renewed interest.

Sound and Meaning. *Can one, in fact, suggest Meaning through Sound?*

Certainly: you may find numerous instances of the successful linking of sense with sound. Analyse one instance, this of Tennyson's in the *Passing of Arthur*. It is the passage where he speaks of how Sir Bedivere—"First made and latest left of all his knights"—makes his hazardous way as he carries the wounded king down the road towards the lake. Read the lines aloud:

Dry clashed his harness in the icy caves
And barren chasms, and all to left and right
The bare black cliff clanged round him, as he based
His feet on juts of slippery crag that rang
Sharp-smitten with the dint of arméd heels—
And on a sudden, lo! the level lake,
And the long glories of the winter moon.

Don't you find there, in the very sounds of the words, a great contrast between rough and smooth? The sounds prominent in the lines about the perilous descent are explosive dentals (*t* and *d*) and labials (*p, b, f, v*) and harsh throat sounds (gutturals like *k* and *ng*). In the first three lines you have six *k* sounds—in *clashed, caves, chasms, black, cliff, clanged*. These sounds—the dentals (formed by putting the tip of the tongue to the front upper teeth), the labials (formed by the complete or partial closure and then the sudden opening of the lips), and the gutturals—are all difficult to make. And the poet cunningly combines them so that his words are in keeping with what he describes. You note, too, the staccato effect—sounds abruptly cut and not gliding into one another—of the first part, contrasted with the drawn effect—"sostenuto", the musician calls it—of the close. And, in "Lo! the level lake, and the long glories of the winter moon," you have the many *l, m, n* liquid sounds,—sounds that, as Ben Jonson said, "melt in the sounding, and are therefore called liquids, the tongue gently striking the roof of the palate".

Spelling. *Why are your Errors in Spelling blamed more severely than your Errors in Language?*

No convincing answer can be given to this question. The fact is so, however; to many, to the majority indeed, you are more to blame for flouting fashion in the spelling of words than for lack of thought or for faults in grammar. The conclusion is clear: though spelling is a convention, a fashion of the time, you had better conform to it.

"Words commonly misspelled" is a title familiar for two hundred years; and examination of the laboriously compiled lists shows how persistent some of the misspellings are. Here they are again. You have, it may be well to assure you, the correct forms only. For the one way to become familiar with the recognized spelling is to observe it closely: to look at the "incorrect" form is to invite errors.

Double or single? is a problem. For it seems that, in the competition for the most frequently misspelled word, *paralleled* and *accommodation* run one another close. To double the last *l* in *paralleled* and to write *accommodation* with a single *m*: these are the errors to expect. If only we thought of *commodity* and *commodious* we should not go astray with *accommodation*. In *harass* an added *r* at times intrudes; and, because we have in *fill full* the doubled *l*, many among us stumble over *fulfil*.

Bus with its plural *buses* might be expected to have a double *s* (like *fuss* and *kiss*): *bus* owes its single *s* to the fact that it is a shortening of *omnibus*. The Latin ending had too much life to be modified. Besides *buss*—meaning *kiss*—was already in the language.

Here is a short list of nuisances in English spelling. Stop at this point, and induce a friend to dictate them to you. If you make fewer than three errors in the twenty words, you are among the "good spellers":

acquiesce, aqueduct, embarrass, committee, moccasin, enforceable, collapsible, inveigle, concede, proceed, disastrous, separate, gauge, banister, disappoint, truly, seize, belief, leisure, desiccated.

Spelling (How Difficulties have Arisen). *How is it that English Spelling is so difficult?*

Tradition, strong in this country, is one reason. Though it is certain that sounds have altered with the passage of five hundred years spelling has, in the main, persisted. Early printers did make efforts to be consistent in their representation of sounds by signs. The representation even then was far from perfect; it was better than it is now. For, whereas the sounds of our words have changed since Caxton set up his printing press at Westminster, the spelling is substantially the same.

Both consonants and vowels vary to an astonishing extent; and a foreigner may well be baffled by the variety. Here, for instance, is the *k* sound. It masquerades in many guises: as *k* (*kiss, king, keen, book, like*); as *c* (*can, catch, come, cup, cruel, secret, claim, act, distinct*); as *ch* (*echo, anchor, school, ache*); as *ck* (*thick, quick, sick*); as *q* (*queen, quit, quarrel, quart, requite, quash, squadron*); as *x*, when it shares a representation with *s* (*example, luxury, six, fox*). In the first seven lines of Wordsworth's sonnet there are eleven *k* sounds, though the eye sees only one (in the word *work*):

> Tax not the royal Saint with vain expense,
> With ill-matched aims the Architect who planned
> (Albeit labouring for a scanty band
> Of white-robed Scholars only) this immense
> And glorious work of fine intelligence;
> —Give all thou canst; high Heaven rejects the lore
> Of nicely-calculated less or more.

Tax, expense, scanty, scholars, work, canst, rejects, all have one *k* sound; and *architect, calculated* have two.

As an instance of inconsistency in our representation of vowel sounds, we may take the long *e* sound. This appears as *ea* in *peace* ("Peace hath her victories no less renowned than war"); as *ie* in *piece* ("What a piece of work is a man!"); as *ee* in *reed* ("A reed shaken with the wind"); as *e* in *sere* ("My way of life is fallen into the sere the yellow leaf").

Consider, too, these troubles in regard to sound and appropriate symbol:

(i) We have words with a consonant symbol without a corresponding sound. Instances are *comb* (rhyming with *home*), *climb* (rhyming with *time*), *ghost* (rhyming with *toast*), *sign* (rhyming with *fine*) *know* (rhyming with *blow*), *deign* (rhyming with *plain*), *scent* (*sent*) *victuals* (pronounced *vittles*), *light* (rhyming with *bite*).

(ii) In *fruit* and *philosophy* are two ways of representing the *f* sound; in *zeal* and *rose* are two ways of representing the *z* sound; in *soon* and *mice* are two ways of representing the *s* sound.

(iii) In *child, fly, height, eye, dye, guise* are six ways of representing the long *i* sound.

(iv) In *she, measure, sink*, the *sh* in *she*, the *s* in *measure*
the *nk* in *sink* stand for three separate sounds for
which the English alphabet has no symbol.

"Split Infinitive". *What is this "Split Infinitive" that many people so dislike?*

When an adverb (or other word or words) comes
between *to* and the verbal part of the infinitive you have a
"split infinitive". Here is one example from an Act of
Parliament: "The Court may decree a dissolution of the
partnership when a partner has been guilty of such
conduct as is calculated to prejudicially affect the carrying on of the business" (Section 35 of the Partnership
Act, 1890). Note "to prejudicially affect". And here is
an example from the Preface to *Alice in Wonderland*: "I
do not believe God means us thus to divide life into two
halves— to wear a grave face on Sunday, and to think it
out of place to even so much as mention Him on a week-
day." Note "to even so much as mention".

It is curious how this fault—assuming that it is a fault
—has become a kind of test: to many in authority a
split infinitive conclusively condemns. Until, therefore,
you have gained an unassailable reputation as a writer,
you had better not split your infinitives. And, indeed, a
sentence in which a split infinitive occurs does usually
grate upon the ear.

Consider the matter a little. In the lines "The Gipsy
crew, his mates, had arts to rule as they desire the
workings of men's brains", *to rule* is the infinitive; and this
is the normal form. That is, the infinitive consists of *to*
followed by the uninflected form of the verb. It needs a
strong reason to diverge from that rule; and the really
strong reason is to make certain that the modifying words
shall be taken with the infinitive and not with another
verb. Almost invariably the modifying words should be
either before *to* or after the verbal part of the infinitive;
the very instinct of our language dictates such positions.
That is why we have such phrases as "humbly to
acknowledge", "so to do", "not to have done" "with
one accord to make our common supplications".

The fact that diligent search will show a split infinitive now and then in writings of the best, is no adequate defence. And in those you find there will, more likely than not, be a sense of awkwardness. There is this (from Browning's *Fra Lippo*) for instance:

> You should not take a fellow eight years old
> And make him swear to never kiss the girls.

It may have been Browning's perversity, his deliberate flouting of fashion, that made him write "to never kiss", when "never to kiss" reads better. And here is Byron:

> To sit on rocks, to muse o'er flood and fells
> To slowly trace the forest's shady scene.

Wouldn't "slowly to trace" be better?

Still, it is not a crime to split an infinitive; and you would not disturb such an instance as in Herrick's *To the Lark*, though a noun is thrust between *to* and the verb. So doing you would throw the verses out of gear. You will enjoy the song. The split infinitive may elude you on a casual reading, but you will find it:

> Good speed, for I this day
> Betimes my matins say.
> > Because I do
> > Begin to woo.
> > Sweet singing lark
> > Be thou the clerk,
> > And know thy when
> > To say Amen.
> > And if I prove
> > Blest is my love,
> > Then thou shalt be
> > High Priest to me,
> > At my return
> > To incense burn,
> And so to solemnize
> Love's and my sacrifice.

Stress in Sentence. *Is there sure guidance to Stress in a Sentence?*

Some guidance there is; but, seeing that custom varies

in the vast English-speaking community, sureness cannot be asserted. Consider the matter: it is quite interesting. The question is twofold: upon which syllable of the word does the stress fall; upon which word of the sentence does the stress fall? The first part of the question is answered below.

The second part of the question is largely a matter of taste. For, quite naturally, we stress in our speech the words to which we would call special attention; and the lightness or heaviness of the stress varies with our purpose. We may in fact make the same words convey several meanings in accordance with the stress. Take the words, "Did you get the problem right?" Put the stress, the emphasis, on *did*, and you suggest a doubt; put the stress on *you*, and you express surprise; put the stress on *right*, and you ask for information. Say "Mr. Smith?" with a rising stress, and you ask a question, "Are you the Mr. Smith I seek?" Say "Mr. Smith" with a falling stress and you assent, "Yes, I am Mr. Smith."

See, too, how you give prominence to a word by stressing it when usually it is unstressed. Stress *a* and *the* in the sentence, "Fox never wanted *a* word, but Pitt never wanted *the* word". You thereby bring out the distinction between glibness in speech and effectiveness in speech.

Stress in Words. *What are the rules of Stress in English words?*

Normally, when an English word has more than one syllable, the stress is near the beginning of the word. Thus you have *báker, dáily, státesman, bédroom, wáistcoat*. But, when a modifying prefix occurs, the stress remains as in the unmodified word: we have *to-dáy, ashóre, forgíve, mistáke*, and so on. At times a variation in stress may show change in meaning: a *gláss-cáse* (each syllable stressed) is a case made of glass, a *gláss-case* is a case for holding glass; a *bláck bírd* is a bird that is black, a *bláckbird* is the name of a species of birds.

The main trouble in regard to stress results from the English tendency to throw the stress forward. This trouble is peculiarly incident to words introduced from other languages. The original stress may be made to conform to English custom; and whether it is so made appears to be determined by caprice. Thus, the adjective *cómparable* has the stress on the first syllable, the noun *compárison* and the verb *compáre* have the stress on the second syllable. The adjective *sólid* and the noun and verb *solídity* and *solídify* show similar inconsistency.

We dislike many unstressed syllables together. This dislike appears to account for variations like *líbrary* and *librárian*, *músic* and *musícian*, *history* and *histórian* *cóntroversy* and *controvérsial*, *órigin* and *original*, *médicine* and *medícinal*, *úniverse* and *univērsal*.

Here are a few words that call for care in the placing of stress: *grimáce, vagáry, advértisement, décadent, despicable, fórmidable, ímpious, revéal, révelation*.

The unstressed part of an English word is likely to be obscured. Thus, though they look different, the final syllables of *nëighbour, dóctor, cólour*, sound the same as the final syllable of *bútter*. This weakening of the end syllables often heralds loss: *fortnight* was once *fourteen-nights* and *butler* was once *botiler* (i.e. *bottler*).

Style. *What precisely is meant by "Style"?*

It must be admitted that many of the definitions of "style" are not very helpful. "Style is the dress of thought," says one; "Proper words in proper places, make the true definition of a style," says another. Perhaps we may be content with "Your style is the manner that is characteristic of you". Applied to language, your style signifies your characteristic mode of expression, having regard to its clearness, its effectiveness, its beauty, and so on.

Macaulay writes, for instance:

The style of the Liturgy did not satisfy the Doctors of the Jerusalem Chamber. They voted the Collects too short and too dry; and Patrick was entrusted with the duty of expanding and ornamenting them. In one respect, at least, the choice seems to have been unexceptionable; for, if we may judge by the way in which Patrick paraphrased the most sublime Hebrew poetry, we shall probably be of opinion that, whether he was or was not qualified to make the Collects better, no man that ever lived was more competent to make them longer.

I will give one specimen of Patrick's workmanship: "He maketh me," says David, "to lie down in green pastures; he leadeth me beside the still waters." Patrick's version is as follows: "For as a good shepherd leadeth his sheep in the violent heat to shady places, where they may lie down and feed (not in parched, but) in fresh and green pastures, and in the evening leads them (not to muddy and troubled waters, but) to pure and quiet streams; so hath he already made a fair and plentiful provision for me, which I enjoy in peace without any disturbance."

You have in our English many styles; and you do not in praising a simple style, for instance, thereby blame an ornate style. Each style may be fit for the writer's purpose.

This little exercise will enable you to realize the wide differences existing among styles. Here are three short extracts, lettered (a), (b), (c):

(a) I suffered the utmost solicitude when I entrusted my book to the carrier, though I had secured it against mischances by lodging two transcripts in different places. At my arrival, I expected the patrons of learning would contend for the honour of a dedication, and resolved to maintain the dignity of letters by a hearty contempt of pecuniary solicitations.

(b) Lo! as I looked back for seventy leagues through the mighty cathedral, I saw the quick and the dead that sang together to God, together that sang to the generation of men. All the hosts of jubilation, like armies that ride in pursuit, moved with one step. Us, that with laurelled heads were passing from the cathedral, they overtook, and, as with a garment, they wrapped us round with thunders greater than their own.

(*c*) I have eaten no vegetables, and only a very moderate quantity of meat; and it may be useful to my
readers to know that the riding of twenty miles was
not so fatiguing to me at the end of my tour as the
riding of ten miles was at the beginning of it.
Some ill-natured fools will call this "*egotism*". Why
is it egotism?

Look at the words chosen: in (*a*) many long-tailed
Latin words in *-tion* and *-tude*; in (*b*) picturesque and
poetic words; in (*c*) words current in the street and
market-place.

Look at the build of the sentences: in (*a*) carefully
balanced, well-girt sentences; in (*b*) loose sentences,
poetic phrases coming impetuously as though to overtake
thought; in (*c*) straightforward, precise, short and crisp
sentences disdainful of ornament.

Now link the three extracts below, lettered (*d*), (*e*),
(*f*) with (*a*), (*b*), (*c*):

(*d*) Cataracts and rapids were heard roaring ahead, and
signs were seen far back, by help of old men's memories, which answered secretly to signs now coming
forward on the eye, even as locks answer to keys.
It was not wonderful that in such a haunted
solitude, with such a haunted heart, Joanna should
see angelic visions and hear angelic voices. The
voices whispered to her for ever, the duty, self-
imposed, of delivering France. Five years she
listened to these monitory voices with internal
struggles.

(*e*) If I had a village at my command, not a tea-kettle
should sing in that village; there should be no
extortioner under the name of country shop-keeper,
and no straight-backed, bloated fellow, with red
eyes, unshaven face, and slipshod till noon, called a
publican and generally worthy of the name of
sinner. Well-covered backs and well-lined bellies
would be my delight.

(*f*) He is surely a public benefactor who finds employ-
ment for those to whom it is thus difficult to find it

for themselves. It is true, that this is seldom done merely from generosity or compassion. Almost every man seeks his own advantage in helping others, and therefore it is too common for mercenary officiousness to consider rather what is grateful than what is right.

[Doubtless you have, easily enough, coupled (*f*) with (*a*), (*d*) with (*b*), (*e*) with (*c*).]

Subjunctive Mood. *A condition being expressed, is it well to use a Special Form of the Verb?*

Probably not unless in formal writings. This special form—the Subjunctive Mood it is called—was once the only correct form for the expression of a condition. You have it in Macbeth's "If it *be* done when 'tis done then '*twere* well it *were* done quickly"; you have it in Hamlet's "Now this, though it *make* the unskilful laugh, cannot but make the judicious grieve"; you have good instances —*fall and die*—in Ben Jonson's little song:

> It is not growing like a tree
>   In bulk doth make Man better be;
> Or standing long an oak, three hundred year,
>   To fall a log at last, dry, bald, and sere:
>   A lily of a day
>   Is fairer far in May,
>   Although it fall and die that night
>   It was the plant and flower of Light.
> In small proportions we just beauties see;
> And in short measure life may perfect be

You have other good instances—*take* and *be*—in Jane Austen's note:

I will not adopt that ungenerous and impolitic custom, so common with novel writers, of degrading, by their contemptuous censure, the very performances to the number of which they are themselves adding: joining with their greatest enemies in bestowing the harshest epithets on such works, and scarcely ever permitting them to be read by their own heroine, who, if she accidentally take up a novel, is sure to turn over

E

its insipid pages with disgust. Alas! if the heroine of one novel be not patronized by the heroine of another, from whom can she expect protection and regard?

We may anticipate that for ordinary speech and writing the subjunctive will vanish. It will have its place only in formal expressions. Perhaps the law, conservative in its language as in its proceedings, will be its last refuge.

Synonyms. *Is it an advantage that English has so many Substitute Words?*

It is a great advantage; for, by this means, you can express the shade of meaning you wish. There are, to be sure, few instances of really interchangeable words; there are very many instances of two or more words having the same general sense. "Synonym" is the learned substitute word for these possible substitutes. *Begin* and *commence*, *behaviour* and *deportment*, *snapdragon* and *antirrhinum* are synonyms.

Consider a few instances: "Deliver us from all sedition, privy conspiracy, and rebellion" says the Litany. *Sedition, conspiracy, rebellion,* are synonyms; but the sedition is a sitting apart brooding over the defects of the governor, conspiracy is a plotting with others against the governor, rebellion is putting into effect such plotting. "Knowledge is proud that he has learned so much, Wisdom is sorry that he knows no more", writes Cowper. *Knowledge* and *Wisdom* are synonymous; but, like the poet, you can distinguish between them. And Fluellen gives you a wide choice:

Fluellen: What call you the town's name where Alexander the Pig was born?

Gower: Alexander the Great?

Fluellen: Why? I pray you, is not pig great? the pig, or the great, or the mighty, or the huge, or the magnanimous, are all one reckoning, save the phrase is a little variatious.

English, having drawn its stock of words from so many sources, is peculiarly rich in synonyms—groups like *proud, dignified, haughty, arrogant, supercilious.* You would not, however, lightly substitute one of the group for another. "The proud peacock", you say, seeing him spread his gay feathers to the view. It is not "the dignified peacock"; he amuses, not awes. Quite rightly you are "proud of your work", proud of having overcome great obstacles. You would be quite wrong, though, if your achievements made you "supercilious", contemptuous of the achievements of others, or "haughty" or "arrogant".

Here are four adjectives similar in meaning, *aged, ancient, antique, archaic.* Look at the sentences below, and you agree that the adjectives are not interchangeable:

   (i) There were forests . . . as the hills.

   (ii) This . . . prince was flourishing in peace.

   (iii) An . . . expression is one that is strange in our times though common enough in times long past.

   (iv) Some people have a great liking for . . . furniture.

(i) needs *ancient,* (ii) *aged,* (iii) *archaic,* (iv) *antique.*

Synonyms being in profusion we do ourselves wrong not to revise our composition: second thoughts may be the better. John Strand's first version—in Barrie's play *What Every Woman Knows*—was, "Gentlemen, the Opposition are calling to you to vote for them and the flowing tide, but I solemnly warn you to beware lest the flowing tide does not engulf you." "The second way is much better," said the critic. And the second way was, "Gentlemen, the Opposition are calling to you to vote for them and the flowing tide, but I ask you cheerfully to vote for us and dam the flowing tide."

Tautology (Pleonasm). *Is a repetition of the one idea in other words always to be condemned?*

By no means always; as we know well, to repeat a thought with a variation may be very effective and give delight. The tautology—the using of words to express an idea already expressed—is a vice of style only when it arises from lack of knowledge of the meanings of the words we use. You could not justify expressions like "I should much rather prefer to walk", (Better cut out either "much rather" or "prefer"); or "pure, unadulterated coffee"; or, unless you seek to summon smiles at the purposed reiteration, "This show is free, gratis, and for nothing". And isn't one or other word in the phrases *recalled back, have got, funeral obsequies, intolerable to be borne, divide up, continue to remain*, a superfluous word? But there is no need to find fault with the peculiarly English way of joining two or more words much the same in meaning—but maybe of differing origins and arousing differing emotions—for the one idea. Phrases like "keep your hands from picking and stealing and your tongue from evil-speaking, lying, and slandering", "acknowledge and confess", "aid and abet", are native to the language.

But look at a little of Miss Jenkyn's letter (you will find it in *Cranford*), and you see an example of a purposed multiplying of words where few would suffice:

The Honourable Mrs. Jamieson has only just quitted me; and, in the course of conversation, she communicated to me the intelligence that she had yesterday received a visit from her revered husband's quondam friend, Lord Maulever. You will not easily conjecture what brought his Lordship within the precincts of our little town.

Don't you think that "she told me" is better than "she communicated to me the intelligence", and that "You will not easily guess what brought him here" says all that the second sentence says?

"That" (Function and Pronunciation). *Why is the word "That" pronounced in more than one way?*

The pronunciation of "that", as of many other words, depends upon its use in the sentence. Read aloud the sentence, "I swear that that is true"; the first "that" has a vowel sound and an accent other than those of the second "that". Spelled the same they are in fact different words: the first a conjunction, the second a demonstrative

pronoun. Read Hamlet's line, "Give me that man that is
not passion's slave": again you have two different sounds
to the one group of letters. You stress the demonstrative
adjective in "*That* man"; you do not stress the relative
pronoun in "that is not passion's slave".

In isolation, that is, you cannot know the sound or the
function of the word: you must see it in the sentence.
Consider these instances:

(i) "Bless us," cried the Mayor, "what's that?"
[Here *that* is a pronoun.]

(ii) I was on my guard for a blow, he was that passion-
ate [In this Dicken's sentence, *that* is a substitute
for *so*: it is a demonstrative adverb.]

(iii) This is the house that Jack built. [Here *that* has a
different pronunciation and a different function:
it is a relative pronoun.]

(iv) I sometimes think that never blows so red
The Rose as where some buried Caesar bled;
That every Hyacinth the Garden wears
Dropt in her lap from some once lovely Head.

[Here *that*, both in the first and in the third line, is a
joining word, a Conjunction.]

Verbs (Transitive and Intransitive). *How do you distinguish between a Transitive and an Intransitive Verb?*

We can best distinguish by considering the work of
various verbs in a piece of good prose. Here is Robert
South's vigorous onslaught on preachers more intent
on showing off than on teaching. The passage is a
capital lesson on the use of language:

"I speak the words of soberness," said St. Paul; and
"I preach the gospel not with the enticing words of
man's wisdom". This was the way of the Apostles'
discovery of things sacred. Nothing here of "the
fringes of the North-star"; nothing of "Nature's
becoming unnatural"; nothing of "the down of

angels' wings", or "the beautiful locks of cherubims":
no starched similitudes, introduced with a "thus have
I seen a cloud rolling in its airy mansion" and the like.
No; these were sublimities above the rise of the
apostolic spirit. For the Apostles, poor mortals, were
content to take lower steps and to tell the world in
plain terms, "that he who believed should be saved,
and that he who believed not should be damned".
And this was the dialect which pierced the conscience,
and made the hearers cry out, "Men and brethren,
what shall we do?" It tickled not the ear, but sunk
into the heart: and, when men came from such sermons,
they never commended the preacher for his taking
voice or gesture; for the fineness of such a simile, or the
quaintness of such a sentence; but they spoke like men
conquered with the overpowering force and evidence
of the most concerning truths; much in the words of the
two disciples going to Emmaus, "Did not our hearts
burn within us while he opened to us the scriptures?"

In a word, the Apostles' preaching was therefore
mighty and successful because plain, natural, and
familiar, and by no means above the capacity of their
hearers nothing being more preposterous than for those
who were professedly aiming at men's hearts to miss
the mark by shooting over their heads.

The *verb* is the part of speech that expresses doing or
being. In the passage *speak, said, preach*, and others
express doing; *was, when*, and others express being.
When a verb is "transitive" it needs an "object" in order
to complete the statement. In the sentence, "It tickled
not the ear", *tickled* is a transitive verb, and *ear* is the
object. In "to take lower steps" and "to tell the world"
the two infinitives, *take* and *tell*, are transitive verbs.
The intransitive verb makes the complete statement.
In the sentence, "Did not our hearts burn within us?"
did burn is an intransitive verb.

The verbs expressing being usually have what is called
a "complement". In the sentence, "The Apostles were
content to take lower steps", *were* is the verb and *content
to take lower steps* is its complement.

Vocabulary (Active and Passive). *What is meant by a person's Vocabulary?*

Your vocabulary is your range of language; in one sense it consists of the words you yourself use to express your thoughts. This is the narrow sense of the word; it is your "active vocabulary". The range of your vocabulary will, it is pretty certain, differ from that of everyone else. The range differs widely from writer to writer. Look at a little of Bunyan:

> After this, it was noised abroad that Mr. *Valiant-for-truth* was taken with a Summons, by the same Post as the other, and had this for a Token that the Summons was true, *That his Pitcher was broken at the Fountain.* When he understood it, he called for his Friends, and told them of it. Then, said he, I am going to my Father's, and though with great difficulty I am got hither yet now I do not repent me of all the Trouble I have been at to arrive where I am.

These are words current on every tongue. Now contrast this of Doctor Johnson in which you have many words you will not hear in street or market-place:

> The notice which you have been pleased to take of my labours, had it been early, had been kind; but it has been delayed until I am indifferent, and cannot enjoy it; till I am solitary, and cannot impart it; till I am known, and do not want it. I hope it is no very cynical asperity not to confess obligations where no benefit has been received, or to be unwilling that the public should consider me as owing that to a Patron, which Providence has enabled me to do for myself

The wider sense of "vocabulary"—your passive vocabulary—is the range of all the words that you understand. Your active vocabulary will be but a small part of your passive vocabulary; but that need not dismay.

You extend your vocabulary a little by acquiring new words; you extend it more by adapting old words. Real or fancied likeness makes the old word seem applicable to the new idea. "Leaf of a tree" you know. You had no trouble, therefore, with "My way of life is fallen into the sere, the yellow leaf". It is an easy transference to a single thickness of paper, "leaf of a book", and thence to figurative expressions like "turn over a new leaf" (mend your ways) and "take a leaf out of his book" (imitate him). We don't burden ourselves with new words when we can adapt the old. This new verb "to bale out" is an instance. We wanted a word to mean "make a parachute descent from a damaged aeroplane"; likening the escaping airman to a bale of goods emerging from the carrying vessel has given us our word.

The learner of English will, very likely, find it harder to grasp variations in the meaning of common words than to acquire uncommon words. How, for example, would you explain to such a learner the meaning of *out* in "Out, brief candle", "He was quite out of it", "Out upon it, I have loved three whole days together! and am like to love three more, if it prove fair weather", "He was beaten out and out", "He was an out-and-out deceiver"?

"Who" or "Whom"? *When should "Who" be used, when "Whom"?*

The trouble arises because the Relative Pronoun is almost always at the beginning of its sentence, and yet it may be in the Objective Case when not "who" but "whom" is wanted. Here are two sentences from Lamb's Essay, *Dream Children*:

My little ones crept about me the other evening to hear about their great-grandmother Field, who lived in a great house in Norfolk. [*Who* is the Relative Pronoun, and is in the Nominative Case.]

Children love to listen to stories about their elders when *they* were children; to stretch their imagination to the conception of a traditionary great-uncle whom they never saw. [*Whom* is the Relative Pronoun, and is in the Objective Case; for the thought is "They never saw *him*".]

Look at the pronoun in these two sentences:

(i) To the English he was a goodly and gallant gentleman, who had never turned his back upon an enemy. [*Who*, the Nominative, is the word.]

(ii) Sir Richard commanded the master gunner, whom he knew to be a most resolute man, to split and sink the ship. [Sir Richard knew *him*. *Whom* is therefore the word.]

We must admit, though, that there is a growing reluctance to use "whom" in speech however careful we are in writing "whom". Both "Whom did I give it to" and "To whom did I give it" are correct and uncomfortable. "Who did I give it to" is incorrect and comfortable. "He wore horn-rimmed spectacles and said 'whom' ", writes one who would describe a pedant.

You will agree that in these sentences *whom* and not *who* is wanted:

(i) Smith, who you thought so highly of, has been appointed. [You thought highly of *him*; therefore, *whom*. The whole sentence would be better as "Smith, of whom you thought so highly, has been appointed".]

(ii) Whom do you say that I am? [It is "Who am I?" and therefore, "Who do you say that I am?"] And isn't *who*, not *whom*, the relative pronoun needed in this sentence: "He could name politicians whom he knew were above such considerations"?

Words. *What exactly is a Word?*

In the first place, a word is a sign made by the vocal chords: we may call it a vocal gesture. In the second place, a word is a sign made by writing, by marks that are understood to represent vocal gestures. Those hearing the word or seeing it may gather thought from it.

The sound, the vocal gesture, may be like the whistle of birds and the cry of animals and may express thought in only a vague way. We can hardly show these words in writing. To express vexation, for example, we may make a click by placing the tongue against the teeth and then suddenly withdrawing it: the *tut!* in writing is a far-off representation. We make a sharp *s* sound to urge on a dog, a soft *s* sound to ask for silence, an explosive sound (as though expelling what is distasteful) to show contempt.

We ask complacence from our readers when we write *ss! sh! pooh!*

Such sounds, often involuntary and meaningless, are not real words. Real words are such sounds as can be combined to express a definite thought.

Words (Choice of). *What Guides are there to the Apt Word?*

Here is a topic of enduring interest. "Many people would have called her a fat woman, but Mr. Polly's innate sense of epithet told him that plump was the word." So wrote Mr. H. G. Wells. We have, all of us, more or less something of Mr. Polly's innate sense; and, when we have written our sentence, we may be quite certain that we have rejected some words and preferred others. For words, though they may be closely kin, are not like the spare parts of a car and interchangeable without loss. *Wide*, for instance, is *broad*; a wide road is a broad road, a wide expanse is a broad expanse; and *narrow* serves as the opposite of both *wide* and *broad*. But the expression for "it's the same thing either way" is "as broad as it is long" (not *wide*); and, being tired out we may, though maybe we should not, describe ourselves as "whacked to the wide" (not *broad*). A man has a broad back, a wide mouth; it is broad daylight and a broad hint, but a wide interval, a wide ball, a wide-open window.

In the sentences below insert the word you think apt:

(i) His hand trembled so much that his writing was almost . . . [illegible, unreadable.]

(ii) There were . . . reasons for the choice. [ponderous, weighty.]

(iii) He should be ashamed of his . . . behaviour [feminine, effeminate.]

(iv) His actions were prompted by a . . . of pity [sentiment, feeling.]

(v) He would not have paid the money except under . . . [obligation, compulsion.]

Doubtless you have decided upon *illegible, weighty, feeling, compulsion*.

Now see whether your choice coincides with Thackeray's: the sentences below are from Chapter LXXV of *The Newcomes*:

(i) He was reserved, . . . , unlike the frank Clive of former times. [Thackeray's word means "not anxious to give news" and has fifteen letters.]

(ii) The founder's tomb stands, a huge . . . emblazoned with heraldic decorations and clumsy, carved allegories. ["Large and stately building", seven letters.]

(iii) This is an old building, a beautiful specimen of . . . of James's time. ["Style of building", eleven letters.]

(iv) The oldest of us grow young again for an hour or two as we come back into those . . . of childhood. ["Places where people play their part in life", six letters].

(v) A goodly company of old Cistercians is generally brought together to attend this . . . ["Formal and dignified address", seven letters.]

(vi) How solemn the well-remembered prayers are, here . . . again in the place where in childhood we used to hear them! ["Spoken out", seven letters.]

(vii) The service for Founder's Day is a special one; one of the psalms . . . being the thirty-seventh. ["Chosen because of its fitness to the occasion", eight letters.]

(viii) I thought the service would never end, or the organist's voluntaries, or the preacher's . . . ["Serious admonition", six letters.]

(ix) Here would be a place for an old fellow, when his . . . was over, to hang his sword up, to humble his soul, and to wait thankfully for the end. ["Active life before retirement", six letters.]

(x) I cannot say but that I . . . in his reasons, and admired that noble humility and contentedness of which he gave me an example. ["Rested satisfied", ten letters.]

Thackeray's words are *uncommunicative, edifice, architecture, scenes, oration, uttered, selected, homily, career, acquiesced.*

And, unless you are weary of what many think a pleasant pastime, see whether you hit upon Milton's choice. The lines are from *Comus*:

(i) Before the starry threshold of Jove's court my . . . is . . . ["Abiding place", seven letters].

(ii) The star that bids the shepherd fold
Now the top of heaven doth hold;
And the gilded car of day
His glowing axle doth . . .
In the steep Atlantic stream. ["Put down", "repress" four letters.]

iii) Listen where thou art sitting
Under the glassy, cool, . . . wave,
In twisted braids of lilies knitting
The loose train of thy amber-dropping hair.
["Letting light pass through", "transparent", eleven letters.]

(iv) Was I deceived, or did a . . . cloud
Turn forth her silver lining on the night. [Black, five letters.]

(v) At last a soft and solemn-breathing sound
Rose like a steam of rich . . . perfumes.
["Extracted drop by drop", nine letters.]

(vi) Along the crisped shades and bowers
Revels the spruce and . . . spring. ["Cheerful", six letters.]

Milton's choice was *mansion, allay, translucent, sable, distilled, jocund.*

Well, what guides the more or less purposed choosing and rejecting? Both the sense and the sound of the word. Look at the word *axle* in the second of the Milton sentences above. We may be quite certain that the meaning was not the sole reason for the choice. The sounds in *axle* bring it into harmony with *car* and *Atlantic* (you have the *k* sound in *x* and in *c*) and with *gilded*, *glowing* and *allay* (the *l* sound in the four words giving a pleasing smoothness to the lines).

A word has a spelling, too. But surely none of us is so lazy or so diffident as to choose a word because it is easier to spell than its competitor. Still, we read in Barrie's *When a Man's Single*:

> The chief reporter was denouncing John Milton for not being able to tell him how to spell "deceive". "What is the use of you," he asked indignantly, "if you can't do a simple thing like that?" "Say 'cheat'," suggested Umbrage. So Stirker wrote "cheat".

For a final instance look at a little of the speech of John Bright, who chose his words with great care:

> I cannot but notice that an uneasy feeling exists as to the news which may arrive by the very next mail from the East. I do not suppose that your troops are to be beaten in actual conflict with the foe, or that they will be driven into the sea; but I am certain that many homes in England in which there now exists a fond hope that the distant one may return—many such homes may be rendered desolate when the next mail shall arrive. The Angel of Death has been abroad throughout the land; you may almost hear the beating of his wings. There is no one, as when the first-born were slain of old, to sprinkle with blood the lintel and the two side-posts of our doors, that he may spare and pass on; he takes his victims from the castle of the noble, the mansion of the wealthy, and the cottage of the poor and the lowly.

Clearly, such a passage is worth close study. Consider it as regards choice of words. "Rendered desolate," says the orator. Why "desolate" instead of "wretched" or "miserable" or "sorrowful" or "unhappy" or "unfortunate"? You answer that the orator sought to lay stress upon the loss of the loved one, and that none of the other words would bring out the idea of loneliness. "The beating of his wings" is the phrase. Is "beating" better than "flapping", "rustling", "throbbing", "sounding"? Yes, you say; none of the others gives, as "beating" does, the idea of a menacing sound. "Spare and pass on", "castle of the noble", "mansion of the wealthy", "cottage of the poor and the lowly"—these and others are noteworthy phrases.

Words (Sense or Sound)? *Which aspect of a word is the more important, Sense or Sound?*

It is an old controversy, whether the sense or the sound of our words is the more to be considered. Here is one that prides himself upon his plain way of speaking and of writing: he considers the sense of the word; if that expresses his intended meaning, he is content. "*Ficum voco ficum*": "I call a spade a spade", he says, "I do not use words for their own sake but simply to convey ideas. I would have you regard not how I write but what I write".

Here is another ever careful in his choice of words, neat in his speech, alert to avoid awkward combinations—combinations like "Burke's works" and "one wonders", —seemingly more concerned about the manner than about the matter of his discourse.

Which of the two is the more sensible? And you answer that neither is very sensible; for both matter and manner must be considered. Try as we may we cannot disassociate sound from sense. The thought to be conveyed is, doubtless, the thing of importance; but, in conveying the thought, you cannot help considering the manner of conveyance.

An old author wrote, "When you see a fellow careful about his words, and neat in his speech, know this for a certainty, that man's mind is busied with toys, there's no solidity in him. As he said of a nightingale, *vox es, praeterea nihil*, a voice thou art and nothing else". Still, it should be our practice—as indeed it was with the author quoted—to give thought to manner as well as to matter, to sound as well as to sense.

INDEX

A or An, 5, 6
Abbreviations, 6, 7
——, plural of, 73
Accent, 7, 9
Adjective or adverb, 9
Adjectives (see nouns, verbs, adjectives)
Alliteration, 10
Allusion, 10, 11
American English, 11
Analysis, 11–13
Apostrophe, 13, 14
Appropriate prepositions, 14, 15
A or The, 16

Cadence (see Rhythm of Prose)
Capitals, 16–18
Case, 18, 19
Circumlocution, 19, 20
Clearness (see Lucidity)
Collective nouns, 20
Comma in enumerations, 21
Comparison (adjectives and adverbs), 21–23
Compound words, 23–24
Conjunctions, 24–25
—— (correlatives), 25, 26
Context, 26, 27
Custom in language, 27, 28

Dash (punctuation), 28
Dilemma, 29
Direct speech, 30
Doubled consonants, 30, 31
Double plurals, 31
Double possessives, 31, 32
Doublets and triplets, 32, 33

E (silent or mute), 33
Exclamation mark, 34

Figurative language, 34, 35
Figures of speech, 34, 35
Foreign terms, 35–37
Full stop (period), 37, 38

H (unsounded or mute), 38
Hackneyed phrases, 39, 40
His or Her, 40
Homonyms and homophones, 41

Idioms, 42
Impersonal verbs, 42, 43
Inflexions, 43, 44
Initials, 44

Interjections (exclamations), 45
Inversion, 45, 46
Inverted commas, 46, 47

Jargon, 47–48, 116–117

Language, vehicle of thought, 48–50
Length of words, 50–52
Like and As (comparisons), 52
Lucidity (clearness), 52, 53

Malapropism, 53–55
Metaphor, 55–56
Mixed metaphor, 56, 57

Name-making (Onomatopœia), 57, 58
Negatives, 58, 59
Nominative absolute, 59, 60
—— case, 60
None (pronoun), 60, 81
Nouns, verbs, adjectives, 61, 62
"Number" of nouns, 62, 63

Onomatopœia (see Name-making)
Over-stopping (punctuation), 63, 64

Paragraphs, 64, 65
Paraphrase, 66, 67
Parenthesis, 67, 68
Passive voice, 68, 69
Personal pronouns, 70, 71
Personification, 71, 72
Preposition, appropriate, 14, 15
——, place of, 72, 73
Pleonasm (see Tautology)
Plural (abbreviations), 73
—— nouns, 73–75
—— (compound words), 75, 76
—— (courtesy titles), 76
Pronunciation, 77, 78
Proper nouns becoming common nouns, 78, 79
Propriety of expression, 79-81
Prose, 81, 82
Punctuation (purpose of), 83, 84

Quotations, 84, 85
Quotation marks, 85, 86

Relative pronouns, 86–89
Report, 89, 90
Reported speech, 90–92
Revision (desirability of), 92, 93
Rhetoric, 93, 94

143

Rhyme, 94, 95
Rhythm of prose, 95, 96
Right word, 96–98

Semi-colon and colon, 98, 99
Sentences (kinds), 99–102
—— (length), 102–105
Shall or Will, 105–108
Should or Would, 109–110
Silent letters, 110–112
Similes, 112–114
Simplicity, 114, 115
Singular or plural 115, 116
Slang (jargon), 116, 117
Sound, 117–119
—— and meaning, 119–120
Spelling, 120, 121
—— difficulties, 121–123

Split infinitive, 123–124
Stress in sentence, 124, 125
—— in words, 125, 126
Style, 126–129
Subjunctive mood, 129, 130
Synonyms, 130, 131

Tautology, 131, 132
That (function and pronunciation), 132, 133

Verbs, 133, 134
Vocabulary, 135, 136

Who or Whom, 136, 137
Words, 137, 138
—— (choice of), 138, 141
—— (sense or sound), 142